Barlow Cumberland

The Story of the Union Jack

How it Grew and what it is, Particularly in its Connection with the....

Barlow Cumberland

The Story of the Union Jack
How it Grew and what it is, Particularly in its Connection with the....

ISBN/EAN: 9783337207175

Printed in Europe, USA, Canada, Australia, Japan

Cover: Foto ©ninafisch / pixelio.de

More available books at **www.hansebooks.com**

RED ENSIGN

WHITE ENSIGN

BY

BARLOW CUMBERLAND,

Past President of the National Club, Toronto, and Supreme President of the "Sons of England," Canada.

ILLUSTRATED.

TORONTO:
WILLIAM BRIGGS,
WESLEY BUILDINGS.
MONTREAL: C. W. COATES.　　　HALIFAX: S F HUESTIS.
1897.

ENTERED according to Act of the Parliament of Canada, in the year one thousand eight hundred and ninety-seven, by BARLOW CUMBERLAND, at the Department of Agriculture.

TO

THE FLAG ITSELF

THIS STORY OF THE

Union Jack

IS DEDICATED WITH MUCH RESPECT

BY

ONE OF ITS SONS.

1. ST. GEORGE.

CONTENTS.

Chapter	Page
I.—The Instinct of Emblems	9
II.—Origins of National Flags	18
III.—The Origin of the Jacks	31
IV.—The English Jack	40
V.—The Supremacy of the English Jack	51
VI.—The Scotch Jack	63
VII.—The "Additional Jack" of James I	71
VIII.—The English Jack Restored	81
IX.—The Sovereignty of the Seas	98
X.—The Jack of Queen Anne, 1707	112
XI.—The Union Jack—The Emblem of Parliamentary Union	123
XII.—The Union Jack and Parliamentary Union in Canada	131
XIII.—The Irish Jack	143
XIV.—The Jack of George III, 1801	156
XV.—The Lessons of the Crosses	166
XVI.—The Union Jack, the Flag of Canada	174
XVII.—The Union Jack, the Flag of Canada	183
XVIII.—The Union Jack of Canada, the Flag of Liberty in America	192
XIX.—The Union Jack of Canada, the Flag of Liberty to the People	203
XX.—The Union Flag of the British Empire	213
Appendix A.—A Plea for the Maple Leaf	227
" B.—Canadian War Medals	231
" C.—A Sample Canadian Record	231

LIST OF ILLUSTRATIONS.

No.		Page
1.	St. George	
2.	Assyrian Emblems	11
3.	Eagle Emblems	12
4.	Tortoise	14
5.	Wolf	14
6.	Cambridge Ensign, 1776	27
7.	Arms of the Washington Family	28
8.	Washington's Book-Plate	23
9.	Washington's Seals	29
10.	Colours of 10th Royal Grenadiers, Canada	34
11.	A Red Cross Knight	37
12.	St. George	41
13.	The Seal of Lyme Regis	46
14.	Brass in Elsyne Church. A.D. 1347	47
15.	The *Henri Grace à Dieu*, 1515.	56
16.	St. Andrew	64
17.	Scotch "Talle Shippe" 16th Century	67
18.	Royal Arms of James I., 1603	72
19.	Jack of James I., 1606	73
20.	The *Sovereign of the Seas*, 1637	86
21.	Commonwealth 20 Shilling Piece	88
22.	The *Naseby*. Charles II.	94
23.	Whip Lash Pendant, British Navy	105
24.	Union Jack of Anne, 1707	112
25.	Fort Niagara, 1759	119
26.	Assault of Quebec, 1759	121
27.	Fort George and the Port of New York in 1770	128
28.	Royal Arms of George II.	133

List of Illustrations.

No.		Page
29.	The Great Seal of Upper Canada, 1792	138
30.	Upper Canada Penny	141
31.	St. Patrick	144
32.	Labarum of Constantine	146
33.	Harp of Hibernia	147
34.	Seal of Carrickfergus, 1605	153
35.	Arms of Queen Victoria	154
36.	Union Jack of George III., 1801	157
37.	Outline Jack. The Proper Proportions of the Crosses	159
38.	The War Medal, 1793-1814	189
39.	The North-West Canada Medal	191
40.	Flag of the Governor-General of Canada	209
41.	Flag of the Lieutenant-Governor of Quebec	210
42.	Australian Emblems	218

Coloured Plates.

I.	1, Red Ensign—2, White Ensign—3, Blue Ensign.	
II.	1, British—2, Italy—3, Greece—4, German—5, French—6, United States	25
III.	1, Grand Union, 1776—2, United States, 1777—3, United States, 1897	30
IV.	1, English Jack—2, Scotch Jack—3, Jack of James I.	65
V.	1, Commonwealth Ensign—2, Cromwell's "Great Union"—3, Ensign Red	88
VI.	1, Union Jack of Anne—2, Red Ensign of Anne—3, Irish Jack	112
VII.	1, Present Union Jack—2, Jack Wrongly Made—3, Jack Wrongly Placed	160
VIII.	Nelson's Signal	170
IX.	1, Canadian Red Ensign—2, Canadian Blue Ensign—3, Suggested Canadian Ensign	176

THE UNION JACK.

"It's only a small bit of bunting,
    It's only an old coloured rag,
Yet thousands have died for its honour
    And shed their best blood for the flag.

"It's charged with the cross of St. Andrew,
    Which, of old, Scotland's heroes has led;
It carries the cross of St. Patrick,
    For which Ireland's bravest have bled.

"Joined with these is our old English ensign,
    St. George's red cross on white field,
Round which, from King Richard to Wolseley,
    Britons conquer or die, but ne'er yield.

"It flutters triumphant o'er ocean,
    As free as the wind and the waves,
And bondsmen from shackles unloosened
    'Neath its shadows no longer are slaves.

THE UNION JACK.

"It floats over Cyprus and Malta,
    O'er Canada, the Indies, Hong Kong;
And Britons, where'er their flag's flying,
    Claim the right which to Britons belong.

"We hoist it to show our devotion
    To our Queen, to our country, and laws;
It's the outward and visible emblem
    Of advancement and Liberty's cause.

"You may say it's an old bit of bunting,
    You may call it an old coloured rag;
But Freedom has made it majestic,
    And time has ennobled the flag."

—ST. GEORGE.

THE STORY OF THE UNION JACK.

CHAPTER I.

THE INSTINCT OF EMBLEMS.

THERE is an instinct in the human race which delights in the flying of flags. Place a stick with a little bit of colored ribbon at its end in the hands of a baby boy, and at once the youngster will begin to wave it, crowing with delight and evidencing every sensation of excitement and energy as he brandishes it to and fro. This is but an illustration of the familiar old adage, "The child is father to the man," for there appears to be something innate in man which causes him to become enthusiastic about a significant emblem raised in the air, whether as the insignia of descent or as a symbol of race or nationality; something which, held aloft before the sight of other men, declares, at a glance, the side to which the bearer belongs, and serves as a rallying point for those who think with him.

This characteristic has been universal among all races of men, even in most primitive times, and in all stages of their condition, whether undeveloped or under the highest civilization.

In ancient Africa, explorations among the sculptured antiquities on the Nile have brought to light national and religious emblem standards, which had meaning and use among the Egyptians long before history had a written record.

At the time of the Exodus the Israelites had their distinctive emblems, and the Book of Numbers (ch. ii. 2) relates how Moses directed in their journeyings, that *"Every man of the children of Israel shall pitch by his own standard, with the ensign of their father's house."*

From the lost cities of Nineveh have been unearthed the ensign of the great Assyrian race, the "Twin Bull" (2), sign of their imperial might.

In later times there were few parts of the continent of Europe which did not become acquainted with the metal ensigns of Rome.

Issuing from the centre of their power, the formidable legions carried the Imperial Eagle at their head, and setting it in triumph over many a subjugated State, established it among the peoples as the sign of the all-conquering power of their mighty Empire. To this Eagle of the Roman Legion may be traced back the crop of Eagle emblems (3) which are borne

2. ASSYRIAN EMBLEMS.

by so many of the nationalities of the Europe of the present day. The golden Eagle of the French battalions, the black Eagle of Prussia, the white Eagle of Poland, and the double-headed Eagles of Austria and Russia, whose two heads typify claim to sovereignty over both the Eastern and Western Empires, are all descended from the Imperial Eagle of ancient Rome.

As these nationalities have been created, the emblem of their subjugation has become the emblem of their power; just as the Cross, which was the emblem of the degradation and

3. EAGLE EMBLEMS.

Austrian.   Russian.
   Roman.
Prussian.   French.

death of Christ, has become the signal and glory of the nations subjugated to the Christian sway.

As in the eastern, so in the western, hemisphere. The rainbow in the heavens is, on all continents, a perpetual memorial of the covenant made between God and man—the sign that behind the wonders of nature dwells the still more wonderful First Cause and Author of them all. Far back in the centuries of existence on this continent of America, the Peruvians had preserved a tradition of that great event which had taken place on another hemisphere; and, tracing from it their national origin, they carried this emblem as sign of the lineage which they claimed as "Children of the Skies." Thus it was that under the standard of a "*Rainbow*" the armies of the Incas of Peru valiantly resisted the invasions of Cortez when, in the sixteenth century, the South American continent came under the domination of Spain.

National emblems were borne on this continent by another nation even yet more ancient than the Peruvians. The buried cities of the Aztecs, in Mexico, are the memorials of a constructive and artistic people, whose emblem of the "Eagle with outstretched wings," repeated with patriotic iteration in the stone carvings of their buildings, has thus come down to us as the mute declarant of their national aspirations. The nation itself has long since passed away, but the outlines of their emblem still preserve the memory of the vanished race.

A living instance of much interest also evidences the continuity of national emblems. Long before the invading Europeans first landed on the shores of North America, the nomad Red Indian, as he travelled from place to place through the fastnesses of the forests, along the shores of the great lakes, over the plains of the vast central prairies, or amid the mountains that crown the Pacific slope, everywhere attested the story of his descent by the "Totem" of his family. This sign of the Tortoise (4), the Wolf (5), the Bear, or the Fish, painted or embroidered on his trappings or carried upon his weapons, was displayed as evidence of his origin, whether he came as friend or foe, and in contest its presence nerved him to maintain the reputation of his family and his tribe.

To-day the Red Man slowly yields to the ever-advancing march of the dominant and civilizing white, his means of sustenance by the chase, or source of livelihood by his skill as a trapper, has been destroyed, so that in his poverty he is maintained on his restricted "reservations" solely by the dole of the people to whom his native country has been transferred, yet his descendants still cling with resolute fortitude and pathetic eagerness to these insignia of their native worth. These rudely formed emblems, whose outlines and shape are mainly taken from the animals and birds of the plain and forest, are memorials of the long past days when their Indian forefathers were undisputed monarchs of all the wilds. They are their patents to nobility, and thus are clung to with all the pride of ancient race.

The instinct in man to attach a national meaning to an emblem, and to display it as an evidence of his patriotic fervour, is all-pervading. The accuracy of its form may not be exact, it may be well nigh indistinguishable in its outlines, but raise it aloft, and the halo of patriotic meaning with which memory has illumined it is answered by the flutterings of the bearer's heart; self is lost in the inspiring recollection, clanship absorbing the individual, claims him as one of a mighty whole, and the race-blood that is deep within springs at once into action, obedient to the stirring call. The fervour of this manifestation was eloquently expressed by Lord Dufferin in narrating incidents which had occurred during one of his official tours as Governor-General of Canada, the greatest daughter-nation among the children of the Union Jack.

"Wherever I have gone, in the crowded cities, in the remote hamlets, the affection of the people for their Sovereign has been blazoned forth against the summer sky by every device which art could fashion or ingenuity invent. Even in the wilds and deserts of the land, the most secluded and untutored settler would hoist some cloth or rag above his shanty, and startle the solitude of the forest with a shot from his rusty firelock and a lusty cheer from himself and his children in glad allegiance to his country's Queen. Even the Indian in his forest, and on his Reserve, would marshal forth his picturesque symbols of fidelity in grateful recognition of a Government that never broke a treaty or falsified its plighted word to the Red Man, or failed to evince for the ancient children of the soil a wise and conscientious solicitude."*

An emblem or a flag is universally amongst men the incarnation of intensest sentiment, and

---

* Lord Dufferin, Toronto Club, 1874.

when uplifted concentrates in itself the annals of a nation and all the traditions of an Empire.

It, therefore, becomes of additional value in proportion as its symbolism is better understood, and its story more fully known; for although of itself a flag is nothing—yet in its significance it is *everything*. So long, then, as the pride of race exists among men, so long will a waving flag command all that is strongest within them, and stir their national instincts to their utmost heights.

CHAPTER II.

ORIGINS OF NATIONAL FLAGS.

WITH such natural emotions stirring within the breasts of its people, one can appreciate the fervid interest taken by each nation in its own national flag, and understand how it comes that the associations which cluster about its folds are so ardently treasured up.

Flags would at first sight appear to be but gaudy things, displaying contrasts of colour or variations of shape or design, according to the mood or the fancy of some flag-maker. This, no doubt, is the case with many signalling or mercantile flags. On the other hand, there is, in not a few of the national flags, some particular combination of form or of colour which indicates a reason for their origin, or which marks some historic reminiscence. There has been, perhaps, some notable occasion on which they were first displayed, or they may have been formed by the joining together of separate designs united at some eventful time to signalize a victorious cause or perpetuate the memory of a great event. These stories of the past are brought to mind and told anew each time their folds are spread open by the breeze.

Before tracing the story of our own Union Jack, some instances may be briefly mentioned in which associations with their history are displayed in the designs of some of the national flags of other nations.

The national standard of united Italy (Pl. II., fig. 2) is a flag having three parallel vertical stripes, green, white and red, the green being next the flagstaff. Upon the central white stripe there is shown a red shield, having upon it a white cross, the whole being surmounted by an Imperial crown. This flag was adopted in 1870, when the uprising of the Italian people, under the leadership of Garibaldi, had resulted in the union of the previously separated principalities into one united kingdom under Victor Emmanuel, the reigning king of Sardinia. The red shield on the Italian flag denotes the arms of the House of Savoy, to which the

Royal House of Sardinia belonged, and which were gained by an ancient and notable event.

The island of Rhodes had, in 1309, been in deadly peril from the attacks of the Turks. In their extremity the then Duke of Savoy came to the aid of the Knights Hospitallers of St. John, who were defending the island, and with his assistance they were able to make a successful resistance. In record and acknowledgment of this great service the Knights of St. John granted to the House of Savoy the privilege of wearing the badge of the order, a white cross on a red shield, upon their royal arms.

So it happened, when the Sardinians came to the aid of their southern brethren, and the King of Sardinia was crowned as ruler over the new Italian kingdom, the old emblem won in defence of ancient liberties was perpetuated on the banner of the new kingdom of liberated and united Italy.

In 1828 the Greeks, after rising in successful rebellion, had freed their land from Mohammedan domination and the power of the Sultan of Turkey. The several States formed themselves into one united kingdom, and seeking a king from among the Royal

Houses of Europe, obtained, in 1832, a scion of the ruling house of Bavaria. The dynasty then set upon the throne of Greece has since been changed, the Bavarian has parted company with his kingdom, and the present king, chosen after his withdrawal, is a member of the Royal House of Denmark, yet the white Greek cross on a light blue ground in the upper quarter, and the four alternate stripes of white on a light blue ground in the field, which form the national flag of Greece (Pl. II., fig. 3), still preserve the blue and white colours of Bavaria, from whence the Greeks obtained their first king.

The colours of the German national banner are black, white and red (Pl. II., fig. 4). Since 1870, when a united German Empire was formed at the conclusion of the French war, this has been the general standard of all the States and principalities that were then brought into Imperial union, although each of these lesser States continues to have, in addition, its own particular flag. This banner of united Germany introduced once more the old Imperial German colours, which had been displayed from 1184 until the time that the Empire was broken up by Napoleon I., in 1806. Tradition is extant that these colours had their origin as a national emblem at the time of the crowning of Barbarossa as the first emperor of Germany in 1152, on which occasion the pathway to the cathedral was laid with a carpet of black, red and gold. The story goes that after the ceremony was over, this carpet was cut up by the people into pieces and displayed by them as flags. Thus by the use of these historic colours the present union of the German Empire is connected with the first union, more than seven centuries before.

The tri-color of the present French Republic (Pl. II., fig. 5) has been credited with widely differing explanations of its origin, as its plain colours of red, white and blue admit of many different interpretations. The present French tri-color has no connection with the French history of Canada. In fact, it did not make its appearance as a flag until the time of the revolution in France in 1789, or thirty years after the French *regime* in Canada had closed its eventful period, therefore there is no French-Canadian allegiance attached to it.

One story of its origin is, that its colours represent those of the three flags which had been carried in succession in the early centuries of the nation. The early kings of France carried the blue banner of St. Martin. To this succeeded, in A.D. 1124, the flaming red Oriflamme of St. Denis, to be afterwards superseded, in the fifteenth century, by the white "Cornette Blanche," the personal banner of the heroic Joan of Arc.

It was under this latter white flag, bearing upon it the Fleur-de-lis of France, that Cartier sailed up the St. Lawrence, and under this flag Canada was colonized and held by the French until the capture of Quebec by Wolfe, when, in 1759, it was changed to the red-crossed flag of England.

According to another story, its creation is stated to have arisen from the incident that, when the Parisian guards were first assembled in the city of Paris under the revolutionary leaders, they had adopted blue and red, the ancient colours of the city of Paris, for the colours of their cockade, to which they added the white of the Bourbon supporters, who subsequently joined them, and thus created the "tri-color" as their revolutionary ensign.

Whether its colours record the colours of the three ancient periods or those of the revolution, the tri-color as a national flag, both on land and sea, was not regularly established for use by the French people until a still later period, when, in 1794, the Republican Convention decreed that the national flag should be formed of the three national colours in equal bands, placed vertically, that next the staff being blue, the centre white and the fly red. This was the flag under which Napoleon I. won his greatest victories, both as General and Emperor, but long before it was devised, or the prowess of its people had created its renown, the French-Canadian had been fighting* under the Union Jack, and adding glory to it by victory won in defence of his own Canadian home.

In 1815, with the restoration of the Bourbon dynasty, the white flag was restored in France, and continued in use until the abdication of Charles X., in 1830, when the tri-color once more took its place, and has since then, notwithstanding the various changes of form of government, remained as the ensign of the European French nation. In Canada it is raised solely out of compliment to the French-speaking friends in modern France. That it has any acceptance with the French-speaking

---

* Defence of Quebec, 1775.

BRITISH

ITALY

GREECE

GERMAN

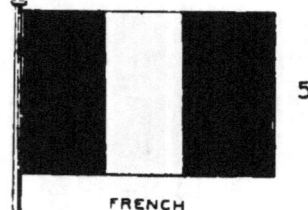
FRENCH

UNITED STATES

Canadian arises largely from the fact that, side by side with the Union Jack, it participated in all the struggles and glories of the Crimea, and the two flags were raised together above Sebastopol as a signal of the combined success of the allied armies of France and England.

These instances of the origin of some of the European national flags show how they record changes of rulers or perpetuate the record of the men or the dynasties that dominated the occasions.

A singularly similar origin is assigned to the creation of the Stars and Stripes, the ensign of the United States (Pl. II., fig. 6).

Troubles had been brewing between the English Colonies in America and the Home Government in England, ever since the passing of the obnoxious Stamp Act of 1765, but although the antagonism had been great, there was no intention on the part of the colonists of severing their allegiance, and under later conditions, there might, in all probability, have been no breaking of the old home ties.

Forces, consisting largely of hired Hanoverian and Hessian soldiers, had been sent out to enforce the objectionable enactments, and hostilities had broken out in 1775 between the resident citizens and these regular troops, but, even then, a change which was made in the flag of the United Colonies was framed not to indicate any change of allegiance, but to evidence the union of the loyal colonies in opposition to the ruling of an impracticable home ministry. So early as October, 1775, Washington had seen the necessity of having some continental flag, which should identify the whole of the forces which had assembled in arms, instead of the military detachments from each colony continuing to use its own individual colonial flag.

An existing colonial ensign was at first suggested by him for this purpose, having a "white ground with a tree in the middle," and the motto, "Appeal to Heaven."*

This was succeeded by a new design for the continental union flag (6), which, on 2nd January, 1776, was raised by Washington over the camp of his army at Cambridge, Massachusetts, being the occasion of its first appearance.

This flag was called "The Grand Union" (Pl. III., fig. 1). It was composed of thirteen stripes of alternate white and red, one for each

---

* "Washington Letters," Vol. I., p. 84.

colony, and in the upper corner was the British Union Jack of that time having the two crosses of St. George and St. Andrew on a blue ground.

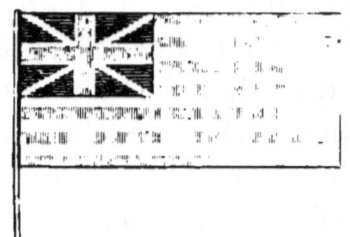

6. CAMBRIDGE ENSIGN, 1776.

The retention of the Union Jack in the new flag was intended to signify that the colonies retained their allegiance to Great Britain, although they were contesting the methods of government.

The first flag then raised by Washington over the armies of the United States displayed the British Union Jack. The source from which the idea of the subsequent design arose we shall presently see.

On 4th July, 1776, the Declaration of Independence followed, but the Grand Union continued to be used. It was not until the 14th June, 1777, or almost a year after that event, that a new national flag was finally developed.

The Congress of the United States, then meeting at Philadelphia, approved the report of a committee which had been appointed to consider the subject, and enacted, " That the flag of the thirteen United States be thirteen stripes, alternate red and white; that the Union be thirteen stars, white in a blue field,

7. ARMS OF THE WASHINGTON FAMILY.

representing a new constellation." A further delay ensued, but at length this flag was officially proclaimed on September 3rd, 1777, as the Union Flag of the United States (Pl. III., fig. 2), and was the first national flag adopted by the authority of Congress.

As Washington himself suggested the first design, and had introduced the second, it is not improbable, and, indeed, it is recorded that he had something to do with the designing of the final one.* However this last report may be, his friends and admirers most certainly had, and the similarity between the design of the new flag and the coat-of-arms of the Washington family points to the source

8. WASHINGTON'S BOOK-PLATE.

---

* "Ross Episode," Preble, p. 265.

of the design. Upon the tombstone in Sulgrave Church, Northamptonshire, England, was to be seen the shield (7) of the Weshyntons, or Washingtons, an old English county family, who traced their lineage back into the fourteenth century.

John Washington, a descendant of this family, had been a loyal cavalier, standing staunchly by his King, Charles I. When

9. WASHINGTON'S SEALS.

Cromwell and the Roundheads came into power, the Royalist Washington emigrated to Virginia, in 1657, bringing out his family and with them his family shield, on which are shown three stars above alternate stripes of red and white. Here settling upon considerable estates, he and his descendants maintained the style and county standards of their English forefathers.

George Washington, the subsequent President, was the great-grandson of the old loyalist colonist. He, too, maintained the old family traditions and habits in the same way, as did all the "first families" of Virginia.

On the panels of his carriage was painted the family coat-of-arms. It appeared on the book plates (8) of the books in his library, and the first commissions which he issued to the officers of his continental army were sealed with his family seal (9).

Thus it has occurred that the stars and stripes of the coat-of-arms of the old loyalist English family, to which the successful Revolutionary general belonged, formed the basis of the design of the new American flag, and through them the memory of the great leader and first President of the United States is indissolubly connected with its national ensign. (Pl. III., fig. 3.)

GRAND UNION 1776

UNITED STATES 1777

UNITED STATES 1897

CHAPTER III.

THE ORIGIN OF THE "JACKS."

It is quite evident, then, that national flags are not merely a haphazard patchwork of coloured bunting, nor by any means "meaningless things." Their combinations have a history, and, in many cases, tell a story, but of all the national flags there is none that bears upon its folds so interesting a story, nor has its history so plainly written on its parts and colourings, as has our British " Union Jack."

To search out whence it got its name, how it was built up into its present form, and what each of its parts means, is an enquiry of deepest interest, for to trace the story of our national flag is to follow the history of the British race.

The flags of other nations have mostly derived their origin from association with a personage, or with some particular epoch. They are, as a rule, the signal of a dynasty or the record of a revolution; but our British Union Jack is the record of the steady growth of a great nation, and traces through centuries of adventure and progress, the gradual establishment by its people of constitutional government over a world-wide Empire.

The origin of the name "Union Jack" has given rise to considerable conjecture and much interesting surmise. The name used in most of the earlier records is that of "Union Flag," or "Great Union." In the treaty of peace made with the Dutch in 1674, in the time of Charles II., it is mentioned as "His Majesty of Great Britain's Flag or Jack," and in the proclamation of Queen Anne, A.D. 1707, as "Our Jack, commonly called the Union Jack."

The most generally quoted suggestion for the name is that, as the first proclamation authorizing a flag in which the national crosses of England and Scotland were first combined, was issued by James VI. of Scotland and I. of England, the name was acquired from this connection: the explanation being that King James frequently signed his name in the French manner as "Jacques," which was abbreviated into "Jac," and thus the new flag came to be called a "Jack."

The derivation suggested is ingenious and interesting, but cannot be accepted as correct, for the simple reason that there were "Jacks" long before the time and reign of James I., and that their prior origin can be clearly traced.

During the feudal period, when kings called their forces into the field, each of the nobles, as in duty bound, furnished to the king's cause his quota of men equipped with complete armament. These troops bore upon their arms and banners the heraldic device or coat-of-arms of their own liege lord, as a sign of "the company to which they belonged."

The kings also in their turn displayed the banner of the kingdom over which each reigned, such as the Fleur-de-lis, for France; the Cross of St. George, for England, or the Cross of St. Andrew, for Scotland, and this banner of the king formed the ensign under which the combined forces of his adherents and supporters served.

A survival of this ancient custom exists to-day in our British military services, both in the colonial and the imperial forces. Rifle regiments do not carry "colours," but all infantry regiments are entitled upon receiving the Royal Warrant to carry two flags, which are called "colours."* (10)

"The "First" or "Queen's Colour" is the plain "Union Jack," in sign of allegiance to the sovereign, and upon this, in the centre, is

10. COLOURS OF 10TH "ROYAL GRENADIERS," CANADA.

the number or designation of the regiment, surmounted by a Royal crown. The "Second" or "Regimental Colour" is of the local colour of the facings of the regiment, and on it are embroidered the regimental badge, and any

---

* Colours of Infantry measure (without the fringe) 3 feet 9 inches long, by 3 feet on the pike. (Perry, "Rank and Badges.")

distinctive emblems, indicating the special history of the regiment itself, thus both the national and local methods of distinction are to-day preserved in the same way as they were originally.

In the earliest days of chivalry, long before the time of the Norman conquest of England, both the knights and foot of the armies in the field wore a surcoat or "Jacque," extending over their armour from the neck to the thighs, bearing upon it the blazon or sign either of their lord or of their nationality. Numberless examples of these are to be seen in early illuminated manuscripts, or on monuments erected in many cathedrals and sanctuaries.

In the eleventh and twelfth centuries, when the Christian nations of Europe were combined together to rescue Jerusalem and the Holy Land from the rule of the Mohammedan, the warrior pilgrims, recruited from the different countries, wore crosses of different shapes and colours upon their surcoats, to indicate the nationalities to which they belonged and the Holy cause in which they were engaged. It was from these crosses that they gained their name of "Crusaders" or Cross-bearers.

The colours of the crosses worn by the different countries were: for France, red; Flanders, green; Germany, black; and Italy, yellow.

In the earlier crusades the cross worn by the English was white, but in later expeditions, the red cross of St. George was adopted and worn upon the Jacque as the sign of England in the same way as shown in the accompanying knightly figure. (11)

The continued use of this cross, and the reason for wearing it is well shown in the following extract from the "Ordinances," issued to the army, with which Richard II., of England, invaded Scotland in A.D. 1386:—

". . . Also that every man of what estate, condicion or nation they be of, so that he be of oure partie, bear a sign of the armes of Saint George, large, bothe before and behynde upon parell, that yf he be slayne or wounded to deth, he that has so doon to hym shall not be putte to deth for defaulte of the crosse that he lacketh, and that non enemy do bere the same token of crosse of Saint George, notwithstandyng he prisoner upon the payne of deth.—*Harleian MSS.*

11. A Red Cross Knight.

The sailors of the Cinque Ports, on the south-east coast of England, by whom the royal navies were in early days principally manned, are recorded to have worn as their uniform in 1513, "a cote of white cotyn, with a red crosse and the armes of ye ports underneathe." These surcoats or "Jacques" came in time to be known as the "Jacks" of the various nationalities they represented, and it was from the raising of one of them upon a lance or staff, in order to show the nationality of those on board, when troops were being conveyed by water, that the single flag bearing on it only the cross of St. George, or the cross of St. Andrew, came to be known as a "Jack," and from this origin, too, the small flag-pole at the bow of a ship is still called the "Jack staff."

This custom of wearing the national Jack at the bow became early established, and was officially recognized. On the great seal of the first Lord Admiral of England, in 1409, under Henry IV., a one-masted galley is shown. At the stern of the ship is the Royal standard, and at the bow a staff bearing the square St. George's banner, the sign of England.*

---

* "The National Flag," Bloomfield.

Such was the origin of the name, and it is from the combination of the three national "Jacks" of England, Scotland and Ireland, in successive periods, that the well-known "Union Jack" of our British nation has gradually grown to its present form.

CHAPTER IV.

THE ENGLISH "JACK."

A. D. 1194-1606.

The original leader and dominant partner in the three kingdoms which have been the cradle of the British race throughout the world was England, and it was her flag that formed the groundwork upon which the Union Flag has been built up.

The "English Jack" is described, in plain language, as a white flag having on it a plain red cross (Pl. IV., fig. 1).

This is the banner of St. George (12), the patron saint of England, and in heraldic language is described as "*Argent, a cross gules*": "A silver (white) field, on it a red cross."

The cry of "St. George for Merrie England" has re-echoed through so many centuries, that his place as the patron saint of the kingdom is firmly established. Wherever ships have sailed, there the red cross of St. George has beeen carried by the sailor-nation, who chose him as their hero. The incident of his adoption as patron saint is thus narrated in the early chronicles. In 1190, Richard Cœur de Lion of England had joined the French, Germans and Franks in the third great crusade to the Holy Land; but while the other nations proceeded overland, Richard built and engaged a great fleet, in which he conveyed his English troops by sea to Palestine. His armament consisted of "254 tall shippes and about three score galliots." Arriving with these off the coast, he

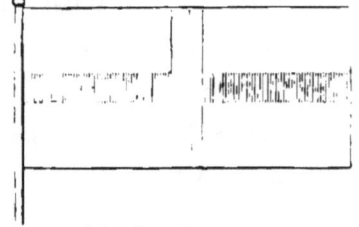

12. ST. GEORGE.

won a gallant sea-fight over the Saracens near Beyrut, and by his victory intercepted the reinforcements which their ships were carrying to the relief of Acre, at that time being besieged by the combined armies of the Crusaders. About three miles north along the shore from the city of Beyrut (Beyrout), there was then, and still remains, an ancient grotto cut into the rock, and famous as being the traditional spot where the gallant knight

St. George slew the monstrous dragon which was about to devour the daughter of the king of the city.

> " Y cladd with mightie armes and silver shielde,
> As one for knightly jousts and fierce encounters fitt,'
>
> *The Faerie Queen*—SPENCER.

This knight was born, the son of noble Christian parents, in the kingdom of Cappadocia, and this St. George of Cappadocia is the acknowledged patron saint of England.

The Christian hero St. George is stated to have suffered martyrdom during the reign of the apostate Roman Emperor Julian, and from his having been beheaded for his faith on the 23rd April, A.D. 361, the day has since been celebrated as "St. George's day." His memory has always been greatly revered in the East, particularly by the Greek Church; and one of the first churches erected by Constantine the Great was dedicated to him.

The form of his cross is known as the *Greek cross*, and is displayed in the upper corner of the national Greek ensign. (Pl. II., fig. 3.)

It is to be noted, however, that St. George has never been canonized, nor his name placed by the Roman Church in its calendar of sacred saints. His name, like those of St. Christopher, St. Sebastian and St. Nicholas, was only included in a list of some declared by Pope Gelasius, in A.D. 494, as being those "whose names are justly reverenced among men, but whose actions are known only to God."*

St. George, the redresser of wrongs, the protector of women, and the model of Christian chivalry, was not a sea-faring hero, but it was after the sailors' victory near the scene of his exploits, that a sea-faring nation adopted him as their patron saint.

The emblem of St. George is said by some chroniclers to have been at once adopted by Richard I. who immediately placed himself and his army under the especial protection of the saint, and introduced the emblem into England after his return in 1194. In 1222 St. George's Day was ordered to be kept as a holiday in England. Others aver that the emblem was not generally accepted until, by Edward I., 1274. This prince, before his ascension to the throne, had served in the last of the Crusades, and during that time had visited the scene of the victory and the grotto of the saint. In support of this latter date, it is pointed out that this visit of Prince

---

* "Sacred and Legendary Art," Jameson.

Edward to Palestine coincided with the change made in their badge by the English order of the Knights of St. John of Jerusalem from an eight-pointed Maltese cross to a straight white Greek cross, and with this appearance upon the English banners of the St. George's cross, but of the English national colour, red*; and that therefore the introduction of the emblem in the flag may have been of Edward's initiation. The same form of cross was placed by Edward I., in 1294, upon the monumental crosses which he raised at Cheapside, Charing Cross and other places, in memory of his loved Queen Eleanor.

From this last date onward the St. George's cross and the legend of St. George and the dragon are in plain evidence. An early instance is that found in the borough of Lyme Regis, in Dorset, to which Edward I. granted its first charter of incorporation and its official seal. A photo reproduction of an impression of this seal (13) is here given. The flag of St. George is seen at the masthead, and below it the three-leopards standard of Richard I. and Henry III., carried by Edward in Palestine during the life time of

---

*(Bloomfield, "The National Flag")

his father. At the bow of the ship is the figure of the saint represented in the act of slaying the dragon, and having on his shield the St. George's cross.

> "And on his breast a bloodie Crosse he bore,
> The deare remembrance of his dying Lord,
> For whose sweete sake that glorious badge he wore,
> And dead, as living, ever him ador'd:
> Upon his shield the like was also scor'd,
> For soveraine hope which in his helpe he had.
> Right faithfull true he was in deede and word."
>
> The Faerie Queen—SPENSER.

Around the edge of the seal is the rude lettering of the inscription in Latin, "SIGILLUM : COMMUNE : DE : LIM," ("The common seal of Lyme"). Near the top may also be seen the star and crescent badge of Richard I., adopted by him as a record of his naval victory, and which is still used as an "Admiralty badge" upon the epaulettes of admirals of the British navy.

This seal of Lyme Regis is said to be the earliest known representation of St. George and the dragon made in England.

Another instance of a later date exists on a "sepulchral brass" (14) placed to the memory of Sir Hugh Hastings, in Elsyne Church, Norfolk, and dated 1347.

In the upper part of the architectural tracery on the brass is a circle $8\frac{1}{4}$ inches in diameter,

13. The Seal of Lyme Regis.

in which St. George is shown, this time mounted upon horseback, and piercing not the fiery dragon of the ancient legend, but the equally typical two-legged demon of vice.

The photo reproduction is from a "rubbing" recently taken from the brass, and shows, so far as the reduced scale will permit, the St. George's cross upon the surcoat and on the shield of the knight.

14. Brass in Elsyne Church, A.D. 1347.

It was under this St. George's cross that Richard the Lion-hearted, after proving their seamanship in victory, showed the mettle of his English Crusaders in the battles of the Holy Land, and led them to within sight of Jerusalem. With it the fleets of Edward 1. claimed and maintained the "Lordship of the Narrow Seas." Under this single red-cross flag the French battlefields resounded with the cry of "England and St. George!" and the undying glories of Cressy, Poictiers and Agincourt were achieved. Under it, too, Cabot discovered Cape Breton, Drake sailed around the world, Raleigh founded Virginia, and the navy of Elizabeth carried confusion into the ill-fated Spanish Armada.

This is a glory-roll which justifies the name of England as "The Mistress of the Seas." Her patron saint was won as a record of a naval victory. With this red-cross flag of St. George flying above them, her English sailors swept the seas around their white-cliffed coasts, and made the ships of all other nations do obeisance to it. With it they penetrated distant seas, and planted it on previously unknown lands as sign of the sovereignty of their king, making the power of England and England's flag known throughout the circle of the earth.

All this was done before the time when the other sister-nations joined their flags with hers, and it is a just tribute to the sea-faring prowess of the English people, and to the victories won by the English Jack, that in its simple form it is the Admiral's flag and flies as the badge of rank: that it is in all the Admirals' pennants, and that the English flag is the groundwork of the white ensign of the British navy.

This "White Ensign" (Pl. I., Fig. 2) is the English Jack, bearing the large red St. George's cross, upon its white ground, and having in this present reign a three-crossed Union Jack placed in the upper quarter or canton, next the staff. It is the "distinction flag" of the British navy, allowed to be carried only by Her Majesty's ships of war, and is restricted solely to those bearing Her Majesty's royal commission.*

Thus has the memory of Richard I. and his men been preserved, and all honour done to

---

* "A penalty of £500 may by law be imposed for hoisting on any ship or boat belonging to any of Her Majesty's subjects any flag not permitted in accordance with the Admiralty Regulations." (See Art. 86, "Admiralty Instns.")

the "Mariners of England," the sons of St. George, whose single red-cross flag has worthily won the poets praise:

> "Ye mariners of England!
>   That guard our native seas;
> Whose flag has braved a thousand years,
>   The battle and the breeze.
>
> "The meteor flag of England
>   Shall yet terrific burn;
> Till danger's troubled night depart,
>   And the star of peace return."
>
> —Campbell.

CHAPTER V.

THE SUPREMACY OF THE ENGLISH JACK.

A.D. 871-1606.

WHILE it is true that flags had grown up on land from the necessity of having some means of identifying the knights and nobles, whose faces were encased and hidden from sight within their helmets, yet it was at sea that they attained to their greatest estimation. There the flag upon the mast became the ensign of the nation to which the vessel belonged, and formed the very embodiment of its power. To fly the flag was an act of defiance, to lower it, an evidence of submission, and thus the motions of these little coloured cloths at sea became of highest importance. The supremacy of one nation over another was measured most readily by the precedence which its flag received from the ships of other nationalities. National pride therefore became involved in the question of the supremacy of the flag at sea, and in this contest the English were not behindhand in taking their share, for the supremacy of the sea meant something more to England than the mere precedence of her flag. It meant that no other power should be allowed to surpass her as a naval power, not that she desired to carry strife against their countries, but more for the protection of her own shores at home, and the preservation of peace along the confines of her island seas.

Alfred the Great of England (871-901) was the first to establish the supremacy of the English flag, and to him is attributed the first gathering together of a Royal navy, the creation of an efficient force at sea being a portion of that policy which he so early declared, and which has ever since been the ruling guide of the English people. The defence of Britain lay, he considered, in the maintaining of a fleet of sufficient power to stretch out afar and prevent invasion before it came too near, rather than in providing sufficient capacity for effective resistance when the enemy had reached her shores. The bulwarks of England were, in his time, as they are still considered to be, her ships at sea, rather than the parapets of her forts on land.

> "Britannia needs no bulwarks,
> No towers along the steep;
> Her march is o'er the mountain-waves,
> Her home is on the deep."

Introducing galleys longer and faster than those of the Danes,* Alfred kept his enemies at respectful distance, and, dwelling secure under the protection of his fleet, was thus enabled to devote himself with untrammelled energy to the establishment of the internal government of his kingdom.

His successors followed up his ideas, and under Athelstane the creation of an English merchant navy was also developed. Every inducement was offered to merchants who should engage in maritime ventures. Among other decrees then made was one that, "if a merchant so thrives that he pass thrice over the wide seas in his own craft, he was henceforth a Thane righte worthie."† Thus honours were to be won as well as wealth, and the merchants of England extended their energies in traffic on the seas.

---

* "Sax. Chron.," 122. † "Canciam" IV., 268.

King Edgar (973-75), by virtue of his navy assumed the title of "Supreme Lord and Governor of the Ocean lying around about Britain," but Harold, the last of the Saxon kings, instead of maintaining his ships in equipment and fitness to protect his shores, allowed them to be dispersed for want of adequate provisions from their station behind the Isle of Wight, and so forgetting the teachings of Alfred, he left his southern coasts unguarded and let the Norman invader have opportunity to land, an opportunity which was promptly availed of.

The Norman monarchs of England held to the supremacy which the early Saxon kings had claimed for her flag at sea.

When the conquest of England in 1066 had been completely effected by the Norman forces, both shores of the "narrow seas" between England and Normandy were combined under the rule of William the Conqueror, communication by water increased between the two portions of his realm, and the maritime interests of his people were greatly extended and established.

Richard I. showed England to the other nations, during the crusades, as a strong maritime power. King John followed in his footsteps, and in 1200, the second year of his reign, issued his declaration, directing that ships of all other nations must honour his Royal Flag.

"If any lieutenant of the King's fleet, in any naval expedition, do meet with on the sea any ship or vessels, laden or unladen, that will not vail and lower their sails at the command of the Lieutenant of the King or the King's Admiral, but shall fight with them of the fleet, such, if taken, shall be reported as enemies, and the vessels and goods shall be seized and forfeited as the goods of enemies."

The supremacy which King John thus claimed his successors afterwards maintained and extended, so that under Edward I., Spain, Germany, Holland, Denmark and Norway, being all the other nations, except France, which bordered on the adjacent seas, joined in according to England "possession of the sovereignty of the English seas and the Isles therein,"* together with admission of the right which the English had of maintaining sovereign guard over the seas, and over all the ships of other Dominions, as well as their own, which might be passing through them.

---

* Southey, "Naval History of England," 213.

During the internecine wars of the Roses, another nationality grew up into maritime power. While the English were so busily engaged in fighting amongst themselves, the Dutch of the Netherlands, under the Duke of

15. The *Henri Grace à Dieu*, 1515.
(From the Pepysian collection.)

Burgundy, developed a large carrying trade, and so increased their fleet that in 1485, at the accession of Henry VII., they had become a formidable shipping rival of England and a thorn in the side of France. Over the ships of this latter country the Dutch so lorded it on the narrow seas, that to quote Philip de Commines, their "Navy was so mighty and strong, that no man durst stir in these narrow seas for fear of it making war upon the King of France's subjects and threatening them everywhere."

Two flags, the striped standard of the Dutch and the red-cross Jack of the English, were now rivalling each other on the Atlantic and the adjacent seas, and thereafter, for nearly two hundred years, the contest for the supremacy continued. A drawing in the Pepysian Library gives the details of the *Henri Grace a Dieu* (15), built in 1515 by order of Henry VIII., which was the greatest war ship up to that time built in England, and has been termed "the parent of the British Navy." At the four mastheads fly St. George's ensigns, and from the bowsprit end and from each of the round tops upon the lower masts are long streamers with the St. George's cross, similar in form to the naval pennants of the present day.* The

---

* These masthead pennants (with the St. George's cross at the head) are worn by Her Majesty's ships in commission. They vary in length from 9 to 60 feet, and in width from 2½ inches to 4 inches.

castellated building at the bow and the hooks with which the yards are armed, tell of the derivation of the nautical terms "forecastle" and "yard arm" still in use.

With such armament the cross of St. George continued to ruffle its way on the narrow seas, and widened the scope of its domain. Cabot had carried it across the Atlantic under the license which he and his associates received from Henry VII., empowering them "to seek out and find whatsoever isles, countries, regions, or provinces of the heathen and infidels, whatsoever they might be; and set up his banner on every isle or mainland by them newly found."

With this authority for its exploits the red cross of St. George was planted, in 1497, on the shores of Newfoundland and Florida, and the English Jack thus first carried into America, formed the foundation for the subsequent British claim to sovereignty over all the intervening coasts.

The supremacy maintained for the English Jack never lost anything at the hands of its supporters, and an event which occurred in the reign of Queen Mary, 1554, gives a vivid picture of the boldness of the sea-dogs by whom it was carried, and of how they held their own over any rival craft.

The Spanish fleet, of 160 sail, bringing Philip II. the King of Spain to espouse the English Queen, was met off Southampton by the English fleet, of twenty-eight sail, under Lord William Howard, " Lord High Admiral in the " Narrow Seas." The Spanish fleet was flying the royal flag of Spain, and King Philip would have passed the English ships without paying the customary honours, had not the English admiral fired a shot at the Spanish admiral's ship, and forced the whole fleet to strike colours and lower their topsails in homage to the English flag. Not until this had been properly done would Howard permit his own squadron to salute the Spanish King.*

The defeat of the Spanish Armada in 1588, under Queen Elizabeth, was one of the crowning glories of the supremacy of the English Jack, but it would almost seem as though the glorious flag had kept for its closing years the grandest of all the many strifes in which it had been engaged in the never-to-be-forgotten action of the undaunted *Revenge*.

---

* Preble, " Flag of the United States."

England and Spain were then still at open war. The English fleet, consisting of six Queen's ships, six victuallers of London, and two or three pinnaces, as riding at anchor near the island of Flores, in the Azores, waiting for the coming of the Spanish fleet, which was expected to pass on its way from the West Indies, where it had wintered the preceding year. On first September, 1591, the enemy came in sight, amounting to fifty-three sail, "the first time since the great Armada that the King of Spain had shown himself so strong at sea."* The English had been refitting their equipment, the sick had all been sent on shore, and their ships were not in readiness to meet so overwhelming an armament. On the approach of the Spaniards five of the English ships slipped their cables, and together with the consorts sailed away, but Sir Richard Grenville of the *Revenge* choosing to collect his men, and not abandon the sick, remained behind with his ship to meet the enemy alone. Rather than strike his flag, he withstood the onset of the whole Spanish fleet, and thus this latest

---

* Monson.

century of the red cross Jack closed with a sea-fight worthy of its story, and which has been preserved by a Poet Laureate in undying verse.

"He had only a hundred seamen to work the ship and to fight,
And he sailed away from Flores till the Spaniards came in sight,
With his huge sea-castles heaving up on the weather bow.

"'Shall we fight or shall we fly?
Good Sir Richard, tell us now,
For to fight is but to die!
There'll be little of us left by the time this sun be set.'

"And Sir Richard said again: 'We be all good English men.
Let us bang these dogs of Seville, the children of the devil,
For I never turned my back upon Don or devil yet.'"

"And the sun went down, and the stars came out far over the summer sea,
But never a moment ceased the fight of the one and the fifty-three.
Ship after ship, the whole night long, their high-built galleons came,
Ship after ship, the whole night long, with her battle thunder and flame.

"Ship after ship, the whole night long, drew back with
　her dead and her shame.
　For some were sunk, and many were shattered, and so
　　could fight us no more—
　God of battles, was ever a battle like this in the world
　　before."

The Revenge.—TENNYSON

In such way, audacious in victory and unconquered in defeat, the English sailors held mastery of the oceans for 700 years, from Alfred to Elizabeth, beneath their English flag, and laid the foundations of that maritime spirit which still holds for Great Britain the proud supremacy of the seas.

CHAPTER VI.

THE SCOTCH "JACK."

From a very early period St. Andrew has been esteemed as the patron saint of Scotland, and been held in a veneration quite as strong as that entertained in England for St. George. The "Saltire," or cross of St. Andrew (16), is attributed to the tradition that the saint had been crucified with legs and arms extended upon a cross of this shape, and, therefore, it is accepted as the emblem of his martyrdom.

How St. Andrew came to be adopted as the patron saint of Scotland is a subject of much varying conjecture. It is said that in the early centuries some relics of the apostle St. Andrew were being brought to Scotland, and although the vessel carrying them was wrecked and became a total loss, the sacred bones were brought safe to shore at the port since called St. Andrews. The most favoured tradition as to the time of his adoption is that it occurred in A.D. 987. Hungus, king of the Picts, was being attacked by Athelstane, the king of the West Saxons,* when Achaius, king of the Scots, with 10,000 of his Scottish subjects, came to his relief, and the two kings joined their forces to repel the invader. The Scotch leaders, face to face with so formidable a foe, and, finding their followers somewhat intimidated, were passing the night in prayer to God and to St. Andrew, when, upon the background of the blue sky, there appeared formed in white clouds the figure of the white cross of the martyr saint. Reanimated by this answering sign the Scottish soldiers entered the fray with enthusiastic valour, and beset the English with such ardour as to drive them in confusion from the field, leaving their King, Athelstane, dead behind them among the slain. Since that time the white Saltire cross, upon a blue ground, the banner of St. Andrew, has been carried by the Scotch as their national ensign.

16. St. Andrew.

---

* Sir Harris Nicholas, "Hist. of Order of Thistle."

Scotch Jack

Jack of James I

III

This "Scotch Jack" (Pl. IV., fig. 2), which is described in heraldic language as "*Azure, a Saltire argent*" (on azure blue, a silver-white Saltire), was the flag carried by the great Scottish national hero, Robert-the-Bruce, whose valour won for him the crown of Scotland, and whose descendants, the Earls of Elgin, still bear his banner on their coat-of-arms. At Bannockburn, in 1314, this emblem of Bruce rose victorious over Edward II. and his stolid Englishmen. Its use was continued in 1385, when the Scots, stirred up, and aided by Charles VI., of France, invaded and despoiled the border counties of England, when both they and their French auxiliaries wore a white St. Andrew's cross upon their jacques, both before and behind, in order that they might distinguish the soldiers of their combined companies from the forces of the foe.*

But St. Andrew's flag was not always victorious. At Chevy Chase and Flodden Field it suffered defeat, but only in such wise as to prove the truth of the warning motto of the prickly Scotch thistle, "*Nemo me impune lacessit.*" ("No one may touch me with impunity.")

---

* Perry, "Rank and Badges," p. 330.

The "Scotch Jack," in all these early centuries, unlike its English compeer, does not appear to have been carried far afield, nor in expeditions across the seas. On land, the Scotch used it mainly as a sign of recognition during the forays which they kept up with unceasing vigour on the neighboring kingdoms of England and Ireland; and at sea, its scene of action was measurably near to their own shores.

Scotland, being so far removed from the fleets of the southern nations of Europe, did not need a regular navy, and never had one; but her far northern coasts, indented with deep bays and bordered by wild fastnesses, adapted themselves admirably to the use to which they were mainly put, of being the lair from which hardy, venturesome freebooters, in those times called "sea rovers," sailed forth in their "talle shippes" (17) and pounced down upon the vessels of the passers-by. The exploits of some of these sailors, under the St. Andrew's Jack, crop out from time to time with splendid audacity in the history of the centuries. One "Mercer, a Scottish rover," during the reign of Richard II. of England, so harried the merchant shipping of England that, in 1378, Alderman John

17. Scotch "Talle Shippe" 16th Century.
(From a painting by Van Eyk.)

Philpot, "a worshipful citizen of London," equipped an expedition at his own expense, and meeting Mercer and fifteen Spanish ships, which were acting with him, brought the whole fleet, "besides great riches which were found on board," in triumph into port at Scarborough. Philpot was haled before the English royal authorities for having dared "to set forth a navy of men-of-war without the advice of the King's Council," but the end justified the means, and the bold citizen, who by his own action had put down the annoyance with which the officers of the realm should have dealt, was let go free.

Sir Andrew Wood, of Leith, who, for a long time, pillaged the English ships and set the navy of Henry VII. at defiance, was another doughty champion of the St. Andrew's Cross.

Growing bolder in his defiance he challenged the English Royal Navy to a contest. The challenge was accepted, and three chosen ships were sent to meet him. These he overmastered, and carried off his prizes and their crews to Dundee, from where, after caring for the wounded and repairing the damages, James IV. of Scotland returned the ships to Henry, saying, "the contest had been for honour, not for booty."[*]

But the greatest hero of them all, the one whose deeds have woven themselves into the

---

[*] Pinkerton, " History of Scotland."

folk-lore of the Scottish race, was Sir Andrew Barton, who, in the time of Henry VIII., not only plundered his English neighbours, but also took toll of the ships of all other nations, without regard to their flag, and made himself the terror of the North Seas. An old ballad tells in quaint style what an English merchant of Newcastle, whose ships had fallen into the hands of Barton, reported among other things to the English Admiral who was in charge of the narrow seas :

> "Hast thou not herde, Lord Howard bold,
>   As thou has sailed by day and by night,
> Of a Scottish rover on the seas?
>   Men call hym Sir Andrewe Barton, Knyte?
>
> "He is brasse within and steel withoute,
>   With bemes on his toppe-castle strong,
> And eighteen pieces of ordinaunce
>   He carries on each side along.
>
> "And he hath a pinnace derely dight,
>   St. Andrew's Crosse yat is his guide ;
> His pinnace bereth nine score men
>   And fifteen cannons on each side.
>
> "Were ye twenty ships and he but one,
>   I swear by kirk, and bower and hall,
> He would overcome them everyone
>   If once his bemes they do down fall."
>
> —*Extract from an Anciente Ballade.*

Sir Andrew was the last of the freebooters, as the rise of the navy of Henry VIII. and the union of the two kingdoms of England and Scotland, by James I., under one crown put an end to these reprisals by the subjects of the one nation on the other; yet it was the remnants of these very rivalries thus engendered between the crosses of St. Andrew and St. George which led to the national Jacks of the two nations being afterwards joined together to form one flag.

CHAPTER VII.

THE "ADDITIONAL JACK" OF JAMES I.—

A. D. 1606–1649. 1660–1707.

The kingdoms of England and Scotland had passed through these centuries of dissension and conflict when at length, in March, 1603, James VI. of Scotland, upon the death of his second cousin Elizabeth, Queen of England, succeeded to her throne, and became also King James I. of England. The nations were now brought into closer contact, and the movement of shipping along their shores increased, as each was relieved from fear of attack by the other. The Royal standard, which bears on it the arms of the kingdoms, is the special flag of the sovereign. And James at once, upon ascending the throne of England, issued a proclamation, instructing a change to be made in its then existing form. Into the flag of Queen Elizabeth he introduced the red lion of Scotland and also the harp of Ireland, which had not previously been included in the royal arms (18), but no change was instructed to be made, nor was evidently considered necessary, in the English national flag of St. George, which continued to be used as previously. Thus, in the early years of the reign of James, the English and Scotch ships continued to use their red cross and white cross "Jacks," exactly as they had done prior to his accession.

18. ROYAL ARMS OF JAMES I., 1603.

Each nation, no doubt, retained a predilection for its own national flag—a preference which its adherents expressed in their own way, and most probably in terms not untinged by caustic references to controversies and contentions of previous days.

Thus it occurred that in 1606, three years after the joining of the two thrones, the king, finding that difficulties kept arising between the subjects of his two adjacent kingdoms, considered it advisable to issue his proclamation declaring the manner in which they were in future to display their national Jacks, and also authorizing a new flag which was to be used in addition to them. This flag was the "additional Jack" of James I. (19).

It is probable that the English sailor had objected to seeing the

19. JACK OF JAMES I., 1606.

Scotch cross raised on the mast above his English flag, and the Scotchman, on his part too, did not like to see St. Andrew below St. George. The additional flag was designed for the purpose of meeting this difficulty, and was ordered to be raised by itself upon the mainmast. As a further precaution, particular instruction was given that each ship should fly only one national cross, which was to be raised by itself on another mast, namely, on the foremast of the ship, and was to be only the cross of its own nation. All controversy as to precedence of the respective Jacks was thus intended to be brought to an end.

This proclamation, as copied from an original issue, in the British Museum, reads as follows:—

"*A Proclamation declaring what Flagges South and North Britaines shall beare at sea.*

"BY THE KING:

"Whereas some difference hath arisen between our subjects of South and North Britaine travelling by Seas, about the bearing of their Flagges: For the avoyding of all such contentions hereafter wee have, with the advice of Our Councell, ordered: That from henceforth all our subjects of this Isle and Kingdome of Great Britaine, and all our members thereof, shall beare in their *maine toppe* the Red Crosse, commonly called St. George's Crosse, and the White Crosse, commonly called St. Andrewe's Crosse, joyned together according to the forme made by our heralds, and sent by us to our Admerell to be published to our subjects; and in their *fore-toppe* our Subjects of South Britaine shall weare the red crosse onely as they were wont, and our Subjects of North Britaine in their *fore-toppe* the white crosse onely as they were accustomed.

"Wherefore wee will and command

all our subjects to be conformable and obedient to this our Order, and that from henceforth they do not use to beare their flagges in any other sort, as they will answere to contrary at their peril.

"Given at our Palace of Westminster, the twelfth day of April, in the fourth yere of our Reine of Great Britaine, France and Ireland, etc. God save the King.

"Imprinted at London by Robert Barker, printer to the King's Most Excellent Majestie, 1606."

This Jack, which subsequently came to be known as the "Union Flagge," was, it will be noted, not intended to supersede the existing national Jacks, for it was directed to be raised on another mast, and to be displayed in addition to, and at the same time with the Jack of each nation. The reason for this use of two flags may be pointed out, a reason which is fully confirmed by the changes made in subsequent reigns.

When James ascended the throne of England, it was his great desire to be styled "King of Great Britain," as well as of France and Ireland. He caused himself to be so proclaimed, and used the phrase in his proclamations, but without due authority. During the first year of his reign opinions on the point were asked of the judges of the courts, and also of the Lords and Commons of England, but the replies of all were unanimously against his right to the assumption of any such title which might seem to indicate a fusion of the kingdoms.

The fact was, that although the two kingdoms of Scotland and England had been joined in allegiance to the same sovereign, who was equally king of both, yet as each kingdom still retained its own separate parliament, their union had not been made adequately complete. The king had particularly desired to complete this union. In a proclamation he issued he states he had found among the "better disposed" of his subjects

> "a most earnest desire that the sayd happy union should be perfected, the memory of all preterite discontentments abolished, and the inhabitants of both the realms to be the subjects of one kingdom."

He says he will use every diligence himself to have it perfected.

"with the advice of the states and parliament of both the kingdoms, and in the meantime till the said union be established with due solemnitie aforesaid, His Majesty doth repute, hold and esteem and commands all His Highness's subjects to repute, hold and esteem both the two realms as presently united, and as one realm and kingdome, and the subjects of both the realms as one people, brethren and members of one body."

But charm he never so wisely, the king could not get his subjects to see matters in the same light as himself. To temporize with their quarrellings, he was obliged to issue the proclamation concerning their flags, but with all his endeavours he could not get their parliaments to unite, and thus it was that each nation continued to retain its own distinctive national cross, which it flew on the flag-staff as the sign of its own particular nationality, and which was, therefore, not displaced by the king's newly created flag.

The construction of the flag itself presents some peculiarities.

In this "additional Jack" (Pl. IV., fig. 3)

of James, the red cross of St. George and its white ground was ordered to be united with the white cross of St. Andrew and its blue ground, the two flags being *"joyned together according to a form made by our heralds."* In this joining the white ground of the St. George's flag was reduced almost to a nullity.

As the form was the creation of heralds, it was made according to the strict heraldic rules of their craft. In heraldy, a narrow border of white or gold, termed a "fimbriation," is always introduced for the purpose of keeping colours separate, where they otherwise would touch, the technical statement of the rule being, "metal cannot be placed upon metal, nor colour upon colour." The white of the St. George was therefore reduced by the herald so as to become only a small narrow margin of white, just sufficient to keep the red cross of St. George from touching the blue of St. Andrew upon which it was laid, or, to be simply "a fimbriation to the red cross of St. George."

The union of the flags resulted in the Scotchman getting, as he usually does, a smart share of all that was going. It is true the two crosses were given an equal display, but the white ground of the St. George's English Jack has entirely disappeared, while the blue ground of the St. Andrew has been spread over all the remaining space. No wonder that an English admiral of the Narrow Seas, hankering after his old St. George's Jack, says a few years afterwards of this new flag: "Though it may be more honour to both the kingdoms to be thus linked and united together, yet, in view of the spectators, it makes not so fair a show if it would please His Majesty."*

This additional Jack of 1606 continued in use, with the exception of the changes made under Cromwell, for over a century. During its term the British kingdom, which had already colonized the mainland of America, from Massachusetts to Virginia, became more than ever an American power; for, under this Jack, the islands which surrounded the coast, namely, the West Indies, Barbadoes, Bermuda, the Bahamas, Antigua and Jamaica, were added to the British crown. On the continent of Europe as well the victorious movements of the flag did not slacken, for under it Gibraltar was stormed, and Blenheim, the master-

---

* Sir William Monson.

victory of the great Marlborough, was won. This was a record on both the continents, worthy of the two races which had joined their forces at its creation.

There were, however, during its century, changes made in its position, which it is well to note.

CHAPTER VIII.

THE ENGLISH JACK RESTORED.

A. D. 1649-1660 AND 1649-1707.

THE new two-crossed flag of 1606 had been authorized to be used by the ships of all the subjects of the king, by the merchantmen as well as by men-of-war. This order caused many heart-burnings among the admirals of the Royal navy, and especially to the Admiral of the Narrow Seas, whose particular right it was to fly His Majesty's ensign on these much-frequented waters, and whose principal prerogative it was to maintain from the ships of other nations the privileges due to the English flag in its claim to the sovereignty of the seas. Under this new arrangement others as well as the Royal ships were carrying the Union Jack at the main, and the officers of the navy felt that their official prominence was thereby much diminished, for how were foreigners to distinguish a merchantman from a man-of-war? Sir John Penington, Narrow Seas Admiral, in 1633, pressed for the "altering the coullers, whereby His Majestie's own ships may bee known from the subjectes." This, he considered, "to bee very materiale and much for His Majestie's honour; and, besides, will free dispute with strangers; for when they omitt doing theyr respects to His Maties shippes till they be shott att, they alledge they did not know itt to bee ye King's shippe."

The Royal navy kept up a constant agitation for the repeal of the order, until at length, in 1634, the thirty-eighth year of the flag from its establishment by James, their claim was acceded to by Charles I., and a proclamation issued.

BY THE KING.

> "*A Proclamation appointing the flags as well for our Navie Royall as for the ships of our subjects of South and North Britaine.*
>
> "We taking into our Royal Consideration that it is Meete for the

honour of Oure Shipps in our Navie Royall and of such other shipps as are or shall be employed in Our immediate service that the same bee, by their flags distinguished from the shipps of any other of Our Subjects doe herebye straitly prohibite and forbid that none of our Subjects of any of our Nations and Kingdoms shall from henceforth presume to carry the Union Flagge in the maintoppe or other part of any of their shipps that is the St. George's Crosse and the St. Andrew's Crosse joyned together upon pain of Our High displeasure; but that the same Union Flagge be still reserved as an ornament proper for *Our Owne Shipps* and shipps in our immediate service and pay and none other. And likewise Our further will and pleasure is that all the other shipps of Our subjects of England or South Britaine bearing flags, shall from henceforth Carry the Red Crosse commonly called *St. George his Crosse* as of olde time hath been used; and also that all the other shipps of Our Subjects of Scotland or North Britaine shall from Henceforthe carry the White Crosse commonly called *St. Andrew's*

Crosse. Whereby the several shippes may bee distingnished and wee thereby better discerne the number and goodness of the same ; Wherefore wee will and straitly command all Our Subjects foorthwith to be conformable and obedient to this Our Order, as they will answer the contrary at their perill.

"Given at Our Court at Greenwich this 5th day of May in the tenth yeare of Oure Reigne of England, Scotland, France and Ireland, Defender of the Faith, etc. God Save the King. Imprinted at London by Robert Barker, printer to the King's Most Excellent Majestie, and by the Assignees of John Bill, 1634."

This proclamation of Charles I. made a very great change in the position of the "Union Flagge" of James, by restricting its use to one class of ships. That it had never been intended at that time to serve as a national flag is again clearly evidenced by the renewed declaration of its being the special signal of the sovereign, to be used exclusively on the ships of the Royal navy. Further, the merchant vessels losing the "Additional Jack" were ordered to continue to use, as of old, their distinctive national flags. For the continued preservation of the peace it was again required that each ship should use only the flag of the nation to which it belonged, namely, the St. George's cross, or the old English Jack, on the English merchant ships, and St. Andrew's cross, or Scotch Jack, on the Scotch merchant ships.

The position of the three flags at this time was thus clearly distinguished.

The Royal Navy ...... The Union flag.
English merchantmen . . St. George's cross.
Scotch merchantmen . . . St. Andrew's cross.

The battle ship *Sovereign of the Seas* (20), built in 1637, was the glory of the fleet of Charles I., and proved herself, during her sixty years of active service, one of the best men-of-war of the time, and "so formidable to her enemies that none of the most daring among them would willingly lie by her side."[*]

The drawing from a painting by Vandervelt, shows the royal standard of Charles I. at the stern, ensigns with royal ciphers on the two masts, and the two-crossed "Union flagge," which, from 1634, was to be the "ornament proper for our own ships," flying at the bow. After fourteen more years had passed away, this royal

---

[*] Phineas' Pett. "Journal," 1696.

standard of the king had disappeared from the stern of the gallant vessels, and another Jack was flying at the bow, while even so early as January, 1645, the headings of the

20. The *Sovereign of the Seas*, 1637.
(From a painting by Vandervelt.)

official lists of the ships of the navy had been altered so that the ships were termed "The Parliament's Ships" instead of being described "His Majesty's Ships."* In February, 1648, the

---

*Hallam.

Revolutionary Parliament of England abolished the office of king, and by this and the subsequent execution of King Charles, cancelled the allegiance of Scotland and dissolved the connection between the kingdoms. A further change was now introduced. The Parliament did not consider the Stuart kingdom of Scotland to be a portion of their State, and ordered that its insignia should be removed from the national flags. An order of the Council of State was therefore passed on February 22nd, 1649, directing that " the ships that are in the service of the State shall beare the *red crosse only* in a white flag quite through the flag," and referring to the carvings of the royal arms, which up to that time had been carried on the sterns of all royal ships, the order directed that these should be altered, and that "upon the sterne of the shippes there shall be the red cross in one escutcheon and the harpe in the other, being the armes of England and Ireland." The form of these escutcheons is well shown in the twenty-shilling piece (21) issued during the Commonwealth. The Parliament also created another flag, called the Commonwealth Ensign (Pl. v., fig. 1), to be carried on their men-of-war. This was a blue flag, having in the fly a yellow Irish harp, and in the upper corner next the staff the St. George's cross upon a white ground.

Thus the Union Jack of James disappeared, and the single red-cross Jack of England was restored to its position as the only Jack carried on the men-of-war of the State.

The merchant vessels of England continued to use their respective national Jacks as before,

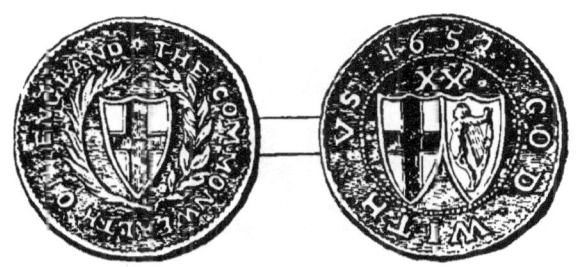

21. COMMONWEALTH 20 SHILLING PIECE.

but the Scotch ships were specially warned that they must not carry either the king's arms or the red cross of St. George, and in case any ships should be met so doing, the State's admirals were ordered to "admonish them not to do it in future."

Cromwell, after he had been raised to the position of "Protector," and had dragooned Ireland and Scotland into submission, put out

COMMONWEALTH ENSIGN.

CROMWELL'S "GREAT UNION"

another flag as the "Great Union" (Pl. v., fig. 2) or banner of the Commonwealth, in which the crosses of St. George and St. Andrew were shown for England and Scotland, and the harp, on a blue ground, for Ireland; but they were all placed in separate quarters of the flag instead of being joined together, while on a black shield of pretence in the centre, he had displayed a lion rampant, to represent his own coat-of-arms and himself.

The great Union of Cromwell did not enter into much use, although certainly it was displayed at his funeral, nor did it take the place of the St. George's Jack, which, thus restored, continued to be used as a single flag until 1660, when, at the Restoration of Charles II., the Union Jacks returned, without any proclamation, to where they had been before the changes made by Parliament.

Pepys tells, in his diary, of how this was begun. Being Clerk of the Acts of the Navy, he had been deputed to read the proclamation of Parliament, which declared the restoration of the king, to the crews on the ships of the navy, appointed to cross over to the Hague and bring Charles II. to England.

While lying at anchor in the Downs, waiting

for the high officials who were to accompany them, he records how the General* of the Fleet went from ship to ship in a small boat, telling them "to alter their arms and flagges."

On 13th May, 1660, being on board the *London*, one of the ships of this squadron, he makes the following entries of his day's doings, and tells how the changes were made: "To the quarterdeck, at which the taylers and painters were at work, cutting out some pieces of yellow cloth in the fashion of a crown and C. R. to be put up instead of the States arms," and records that he had also attended "in the afternoon a council of war only to acquaint them that the harp must be taken out of all their flags, it being very offensive to the king."

After the Restoration, the subjects of the king evidently began, in their enthusiasm, to make indiscriminate use of the Union Jack, for they needed, a few years afterwards, to be reminded of the special instructions which had been given in the previous reign, so that in 1663, under Charles II., another proclama-

---

* Under the Commonwealth successful generals had been appointed to commands as admirals in the navy, but they still retained their military titles.

tion was issued, from which the following extract is made:

> "*A proclamation for the regulating the colours to be worn on merchant ships.—Charles R.*
>
> "Whereas by ancient usage no merchants' ships ought to bear the Jack, which is for distinction appointed for His Majesty's ships.
>
> "His Majesty strictly charges and commands all his subjects, that from henceforth they do not presume to wear *His Majesty's Jack*, commonly called the Union Jack, on any of their ships or vessels, without particular warrant for their so doing from His Majesty, or the Lord High Admiral of England. And His Majesty doth further command all his loving subjects without such warrant they presume not to wear on board their ships or vessels any Jacks made in imitation of His Majesty's, or any other flags, Jacks or ensigns whatsoever, than those usually heretofore worn on merhants' ships, viz., the flag and *Jack white*, with a red cross, commonly called St. George's cross, passing quite through the same, and the *En-*

sign red with the like cross in a canton white at the upper corner thereof next to the staff."

The distinctive order of the flags was this time arranged to be:

Royal Navy—
    The "Commonly Called" Union Jack.
Merchantmen—
    I. The "Jack White," or plain St. George's Jack.
    II. The "Ensign Red," or red flag, with the "Jack White" in the upper corner.

From the time of this proclamation of Charles II. the Jack of James regained a partial position, but only as a single flag, and even then was ordered to be used only on the royal men-of-war. The merchant ships, however, began again so frequently to fly it, instead of their single cross Jacks, that in the reign of William III., and again in the reign of Queen Anne (prior to the creation of her own three-cross Jack) it was found necessary to issue special proclamations reiterating the official restriction of this Jack of James to the ships of the royal navy, and forbidding any other ships to use it.

Having traced the Jack we may note the changes in the standard. Under James I. and Charles I. the flag flown at the stern of the men-of-war had been the royal standard of the king (see *Sovereign of the Seas*). At the time of the Commonwealth the ships of the navy were no longer the ships of the sovereign, but were the ships of the State. It was to take the place of this standard at the stern that the "Commonwealth ensign" had been designed. In this paramount flag Parliament placed the St. George's cross, in 1649, when they ordered the single English Jack to take the place of the two crossed "additional" Jack of James I.

The ensign is stated to have been at first intended only as an admiral's flag, to be flown by the Admiral of the blue. The colour of the field upon which the Irish harp was first placed was blue, but afterwards it was more generally adopted in the red flags, as well as in the blue,* red being the colour of England. When, therefore, the harp had been removed from "all" their flags there remained the simple "ensign red," having the St. George's cross in the upper white canton.

---

* Laughton, "Heraldry of the Sea."

The drawing of the *Naseby* (22), on which Charles II. came to England at the time of his Restoration, in 1660, shows this red ensign flying at the stern. There was not sufficient time for the making of new flags and standards,

22. THE *Naseby*. CHARLES II.
(From a painting by Vandervelt.)

therefore those which they had in use were altered on board the ships, as Pepys has told, before crossing over to the Hague, and this flag is most probably a Parliamentary "Ensign Red," with the Irish harp cut out (Pl. v., fig. 3).

A very great deal of dependance cannot be

placed on the form of the flags introduced into their pictures by artists even of highest rank. When painting flags more attention is given to the colour effect desired to be produced than to the accurate drawing of their details.

Some instances of unworthy errors in national flags may be mentioned. On one series of the national bank-notes issued by the United States Government a representation is shown of "Washington crossing the Delaware," on December 25, 1776. In this the flag with stars and stripes is prominently shown, although no such flag had any existence until a year and a half afterwards. In the Capitol of the United States there is a picture of the "Battle of Lake Erie," fought in 1814, in which the flag on Commodore Perry's boat has only thirteen stars and thirteen stripes, although the United States flag had been changed twenty years before, in 1794, to have fifteen stars and fifteen stripes. On the walls of the "Commons Corridor" in the British Houses of Parliament at Westminster, is a fresco representing the landing of Charles II., in 1660, in which the Union Jack is depicted as having three crosses, the red cross of St. Patrick being included, although it was not entered in the flag until 1801, or 140 years afterwards.

In each of these instances the artist was painting from imagination, but the picture from which our illustration of the *Naseby* is taken, was painted by Vandervelt, who was himself present on the occasion he recorded, and, seeing that he was the most celebrated marine artist of his day, the details of the flags may be taken to be correct.

The proclamation of 1663 shows that not only royal ships, but also all merchant ships were flying the "ensign red" at the stern in the same way as on the *Naseby*, and thus this flag became established as the national ensign.

The place of distinction at the stern had been occupied, as under Charles I., by the royal standard of the reigning king; to this position the Commonwealth ensign had been installed as being the ensign of Parliament, and then by the unpremeditated transition at the "Restoration" the red ensign succeeded to the post of honour as the ensign of the nation.

The story of this flag exemplifies the same peculiar genius as is shown in the British constitution, for it attained to its position, not by a single verbal enactment, but by the force of unwritten usage and the gradual acceptance of the will of the people.

The St. George's cross had been placed in the upper corner of the Commonwealth ensign; from here it had passed into the ensign red of Charles II., thereafter borne at the stern on both merchantmen and men-of-war. In the paramount ensign of the nation, the single cross English Jack was therefore carried unchanged from 1649 to 1707, when its place in the national ensign was taken *for the first time* by a two-crossed Jack, and then only by the first *real* Union Jack, the Jack of Queen Anne.

In all these series of changes it is directly evidenced that the *commonly called* "Union Jack" of James was only an "additional" flag, that it was "exceptional," and had not officially superseded the local national Jacks, and that it had never been introduced into the paramount or national ensign of the nation.

7

CHAPTER IX.

THE SOVEREIGNTY OF THE SEAS.

At the close of the first historic period of the St. George's Jack we have seen it reigning supreme upon the seas around the shores of England. The great Armada had, in 1588, been met and shattered, and its squadrons so relentlessly pursued around the British Isles that but a remnant remained to struggle back to Spain, and tell the story of their defeat.

After such a victory as this, the red cross flag of the "Navie Royall," sailed the Narrow Seas with more assurance than ever, claiming and receiving the obeisance of all vessels that were passing by. The ancient policy of Alfred and of John had been as much esteemed during this Elizabethan period, and its principles adhered to for the same reason as in the earliest days, but the increase of merchant shipping and the rise of the business fleets of

England now gave a new reason for its being maintained beyond the old one of self-defence. Riches were now to be found beyond the confines of these narrow seas. Sir Walter Raleigh stated the new reason with a terseness which four centuries of phrasemaking has not since excelled. Said he: "Whosoever commands the sea, commands the trade; whosoever commands the trade of the world, commands the riches of the world, and consequently the world itself."

The sovereignty of the seas had in this way developed a monetary value; yet, whatever may have been their underlying causes, the contests for the supremacy which, for the next hundred years, kept simmering between the nations, bursting out now and then into blasts of open war, arose ostensibly from disputes between the guardians of the fleets regarding the precedence of their respective flags.

The sea rovers of Elizabeth had developed into something very like "gentleman-buccaneers." They ranged the oceans, preying upon the Spanish and Portuguese ships wherever they were to be found, and returned in joyousness, bringing home their booty. The maritime eagerness of the people was whetted by these prizes, and it is said that even the Queen herself was not averse to accepting from her good subjects, Drake and Hawkins, a share of the proceeds of their prowess. The reign of the Jack of James I. had scarce begun, when a neighbouring maritime rival arose to assume formidable proportions. Nurtured in the hardy school of their fishing fleets, the Dutch merchantmen not only copied the English methods of preying abroad on the ships of other nations, but also began to employ themselves actively in carrying the business of their own merchants, and next, which was an intrusion much more objectionable, to enter into competition with the English ships in carrying the merchandise of the other nations of Europe. Thus the passage of their fleets along the coasts of England greatly increased. As soon as the Spanish war was over, Sir William Monson, the Admiral of the Narrow Seas, demanded that the ships of all other nations should, as of old, lower their flags in the presence of his own, "a courtesy which could not," he said, "be challenged by right, but now that the war was ended, His Majesty, James I. demanded the full recognition of such rights and duties as belonged to his predecessors."* These rights he accordingly proceeded to enforce. The "rufflings" increased in frequency, and the contest went merrily on, as the Dutch, increasing in enterprise and volume of shipping, chafed under the domination of the English admirals. In this restlessness they were encouraged by the differences raging in the next reign between King Charles I. and his Parliament. These latter thwarted the king's efforts at sea, and refused to contribute any ship-money, declaring it to be an insufferable tax; while he, without their concurrence, was attempting to strengthen the navy he had created for the protection of his shores, by maintaining the old English policy. The king's sailors felt keenly the increasing insolence of the passing Dutch ships, as wrote one old salt: "What affront can be greater, or what can make a man valianter, than a dishonour done to prince and country, especially by a people that was wont to know no more than how to catch, pickle, and feed fish.†

Notwithstanding the Parliament's objection, a navy was at one time collected of sufficient strength that, when the Dutch and French fleets joined together with the avowed

---

* Munson's "Naval History of England." † Monson.

intention of contesting the command of the sea, its simply sailing out to meet them overawed their forces, as reports Monson: "It is to be observed that the greatest threateners are the least fighters; and so it fared with them; for they no sooner heard of our readiness to find them, but they plucked in their horns and quitted our coast, never more repairing to it."

The King's opponents said the quarrels with the Dutch over the honour due to the flag were fomented only for the purpose of forming an excuse for extorting money by the objectionable tax, whose proceeds, they alleged, were expended for other purposes. So the people resisted while the King insisted, and meanwhile the Dutch maritime power continued to grow. The struggle between the Parliament and the King resulted in the defeat and execution of Charles, and the weakening of the fleet brought on the humiliation of the English flag, by Van Tromp, who, during the first Dutch war, triumphantly carried a broom at his masthead, as a sign that the Dutch had swept the English flag from the Narrow Seas.

Under Cromwell, in 1653, the St. George's cross had been restored.

The Council of State took heart, and showed by their actions that once more the homage due the national flag was held by them in as great esteem as it had been by the King and his party in the royal days. The orders to their naval commanders were explicit:

> "And whereas the dominion of these seas has, time out of mind, undoubtedly belonged to this nation, and the ships of all other nations, in acknowledgment of that dominion, have used to take down their flags upon sight of the Admiral of England and not to bear it in his presence, you are, as much as in you lies, to endeavour to preserve the dominion of the sea, and to cause the ships of all other nations to strike their flags and not to bear them up in your presence, and to compel such as are refractory therein by seizing their ships and sending them to be punished, according to the Laws of the Sea, unless they yield obedience and make such repair as you approve."*

Von Tromps' glory was of but short duration, for the Roundhead dragoon Blake,

---

* Bloomfield, "The National Flag," p. 186.

nicknamed "the cavalryman at sea," soon clipped his wings. In return for the compliments of the previous year, Blake, after his victory, ran a pennant up on his mast, long and narrow like a whip-lash, to show that he had in his turn driven the Dutchman off the seas. Peace followed in 1654. In this treaty of peace the Dutch agreed that:

> "The ships of the Dutch, as well in ships of war as others, meeting any of the ships of war of the English Commonwealth in the British seas, shall strike their flags and lower their topsail in such manner as hath ever been at any time heretofore practised under any form of government."

Thus had the old sea supremacy of the nation of England, claimed by King John, been again acknowledged, but on this occasion was, for the first time, accorded to England by the terms of a formal treaty.

It was the red-cross Jack of St. George introduced by Richard I., and raised as his "Royal Flag" by King John, which had in previous times received the honour of the "Sovereign Lordship of the seas." We have seen how, for a while, its place had been shared by the additional two-crossed Jack of James, but now, by the incident of the temporary dissolution with Scotland under the Commonwealth, the English Jack was once more reigning in sole possession of the flag-staff, to receive by the terms of this treaty the renewal of that proud homage which its single red cross had received four centuries before. It was a happy coincidence which the flag of the sea-faring Englishman most fully deserved,

23. WHIP-LASH PENDANT—BRITISH NAVY.

and the whip-lash masthead pendants with the St. George's cross in the white ground at the head (23) borne on all Her Majesty's ships in commission preserve the story of this exploit to the present day.

Notwithstanding this check, the marine power, both naval and merchant of the Dutch kept on increasing. They had challenged the English merchantman, and become the general carriers for all Europe. The Commonwealth of England, in self-defence, enacted a navigation law that all produce imported into the kingdom of Britain, should be carried either in English ships or in those of the country whence the cargo was obtained.

It was the contest for the money value of the "command" of the sea which was really being waged, and the commerce of distant continents was the prize which would fall to the victors' share. Vessels of the Dutch and other nations were ordered to heave to, or were stopped by a shot across their bows, not only to compel observance of the supremacy of the flag, but also to search their holds for goods which the searchers might consider should have been carried in English ships.

Soon another Dutch war blazed out under Charles II., 1665-67. De Ruyter sailed up the Thames to Tilbury, but again the success was but temporary, for at the close of the war "New Amsterdam," in America, and the command of the Hudson River, was ceded to the English. The name of the new territory then obtained, was changed to New York, in honour of the Duke of York, the King's brother, which English and royal name it still retains, although now forming the principal maritime city of the Republic of the United States. With the booty came, in the articles of peace, the old-time ascription of sovereignty to the British flag. It was again agreed by one of the articles:

> "That the ships and vessels of the so United Provinces, as well men-of-war as others, meeting any man-of-war of the said King of Great Britain in the British seas, shall strike their flag and lore the topsail in such manner as the same hath been formally observed in any times whatsoever."*

But the rivalry between the flags was too intense to continue much longer without coming to a definite climax. The "command" foreseen by Raleigh was at stake. Both nations had the maritime instinct, and both the genius of colonizing power, so that one or the other of them must give place, and leave to the survivor the supreme possession of all that this command implied. Thus the third and final war came on (1672-74).

The fighting flag of the English navy of the day, the red ensign, was flying at the

---
* Treaty of Breda, 1667.

fore on the men-of-war as the signal to "engage the enemy," and at the stern of both men-of-war and merchantmen as the national ensign. While the Royal navy was battling with its guns, the merchant navy of England was cutting into the carrying trade of the Dutch. So that at the close of the war the British merchant ships had captured the greater part of the foreign business of the enemy, and by thus exhausting the earnings, and reducing the fighting resources of the Dutch, contributed to the final victory almost equally with the exploits of the men-of-war.

The contest, although short, was sharp. The strife had been for the merchant carrying trade of the world, and when it was won whole colonies were transferred with it to the victorious English.

During the interval which had followed the previous war the English had given New York to the Dutch in exchange for Guiana, but now they took both of them back.* These countries formed only a portion of the victor's spoil. Above all these and other

---

*The boundaries of the territories then transferred formed the subject of the recent Venezuela excitement.

great money results, the old sea spirit again asserted itself, and setting into inferior position the additions to the realm, or the compensations exacted for the expenses of the war, the final treaty declares among its first clauses the lordly renewal of the centuries old right of the respect and salute due to the nation's flag!

> "In due acknowledgment on their part, the King of Great Britain's right to have his flag respected in the seas hereafter mentioned, shall and do declare and agree, that whatever ships or vessels belonging to the said United Provinces, whether vessels of war or others, or whether single or in fleets, shall meet in any of the seas from Cape Finisterre to the middle point of the land Van Staten, in Norway, with any ships or vessels belonging to His Majesty of Great Britain, whether these ships be single or in great number, if they carry His Majesty's of Great Britain flag or Jack, the aforesaid Dutch vessels or ships shall strike their flag and lower their topsail in the same manner and with as much respect as hath at any time, or in any place,

been formerly practised towards any ships of His Majesty of Great Britain or his predecessors, by any ships of the States General or their predecessors."*

The Jack of His Majesty Charles II. was the two-crossed "additional" Jack of his father, restored to the navy at the Restoration, and is shown on the *Naseby* (22).

The Jack flies at the bow, and on the mizzen; the admiralty flag is at the fore; the royal standard at the main, but at the stern is the sign of nationality, the "ensign red" with the St. George's cross.

This red ensign was the flag which the ships of that royal navy bore when they won the final supremacy of the sea from the navy of Holland. It was the flag of the British merchant navy of the time, and above them signalled that other command, which was then won from the Dutch "the command of the trade, which is the command of the riches of the world." To this victory the merchantman, by his seamanship and energy, had done his full share, and therefore at this present day the merchant ships of Britain

---

* Treaty of Westminster, Charles II. and Holland, 1674.

bear the red ensign on every sea and in every clime, in rightful acknowledgment of the part he played in gaining the supremacy of the sea.

This supremacy, and still more the spirit of supremacy, has ever since remained dominant in the British heart. The British navy and the British merchant marine, each of them surpass in number and in power the combined navies and ships of any other nations on the globe, and thus with lusty throats her children boldly sing,

"*Rule Britannia ;*
Britannia rules the waves."

CHAPTER X.

THE JACK OF QUEEN ANNE, 1707.

THE FIRST UNION JACK.

In the year 1707, being the sixth year of the reign of Queen Anne, the parliaments of England and Scotland were at length brought into union in one parliament. Up to this time there had not been one distinctive "Union Jack" to represent both the kingdoms, no one flag taking the place of the separate national Jacks of St. George and St. Andrew, which the English or Scotch subjects of the sovereign had always continued to use, according to their nationality. Immediately after the union of the two parliaments, Queen Anne issued her proclamation

24. UNION JACK OF ANNE, 1707.

UNION JACK OF ANNE.

RED ENSIGN OF ANNE

IRISH JACK

creating "Our Jack" as the *sole* ensign armorial of the now completely united kingdoms of Great Britain and of the dominions under its rule. The flag thus authorized was the first Union Jack (24).

ROYAL ARMS.

With three fleur-de-lis quartered in the seconds, and the motto "Semper Eadem."

BY THE QUEEN.

A Proclamation — Declaring what ensign or colours shall be worn at sea in merchant ships or vessels belonging to any of Her Majesty's subjects of Great Britain and the Dominions thereunto belonging. —Anne R.

"Whereas, by the first article of the Treaty of Union, as the same hath been ratified and approved by several Acts of Parliament, the one made in our Parliament of England, and the other in our Parliament of Scotland, it was provided and agreed that the ensigns armorial of our Kingdom of Great Britain be such as we should appoint, and the crosses of Saint George and Saint Andrew conjoyned in such manners as we should think fit, and used in all flags, banners, standards and ensigns, both at sea and land, we have therefore thought fit, by and with the advice of our Privy Council, to order and appoint the ensign described on the side or margent hereof, to be worn on board all ships or vessels belonging to any of our subjects whatsoever, and to issue this, our Royal Proclamation, to notifie the same to all our loving subjects, hereby strictly charging and commanding the masters of all merchant ships and vessels belonging to our subjects, whether employed in our service or otherwise, and all other persons whom it may concern, to wear the said ensign on board the ships or vessels."

After creating the ensign which was to be used by all ships, warning was given against the using of any of the distinctive flags of the royal navy without permission.

"And whereas divers of our subjects have presumed on board their ships to wear our flag, Jacks and pendants, which according to ancient usage, have been appointed as a distinction for our ships, and have worn flags, Jacks and pendants in shape and mixture of colours so little different from ours, as not without difficulty to be distinguished therefrom. We do therefore, with the advice of our Privy Council, hereby strictly charge and command all our subjects whatsoever, that they do not presume to wear in any of their ships our Jack, commonly called the Union Jack, nor any pendants, nor any such colours as are usually worn by our ships without particular warrant for their so doing from us."

The proclamation then stated that no other ensign was to be used, and that the new ensign was to take the place of the ensign up to that time used by merchant ships.

"And do hereby further command all our loving subjects that without such warrant as aforesaid they presume not to wear on board their ships any other ensign than the ensign described on the side or margent hereof, which shall be worn instead of the ensign before this time usually worn on merchant ships.

"Given at our Court at Windsor, the 28th day of July, in the sixth year of our reign.

"*God Save the Queen.*"

Here, then, we have the establishment of a new flag in accordance with the intention of the Treaty of Union, which had received the separate approval of the Parliament of England, and of the Parliament of Scotland, before either had passed out of existence and become merged in the new " Union " Parliament. In this flag the crosses of St. George and St. Andrew were conjoined, the new flag was called " Our Jack " (Pl. vi., fig. 1), which, as a " Union Jack," was to be used as part of all flags, banners and ensigns, both at sea and land, but in its simple form, as a simple Jack, was not to be used afloat on any other ships than Her Majesty's royal navy without particular warrant.

We have seen how, in 1660, the two-crossed Jack of James had come back into use only in addition to the two national crosses, and how the St. George's cross had been left in possession of the upper corner of the " red ensign."

A notable change was now made. Although the St. George's cross remained, as it still does, in the admiral's pendant, its place in the upper corner of the red ensign was now taken by the new " Union Jack," in the form as shown " in the margent " (Pl. vi., fig. 2).

The "red ensign" thus formed, was thereafter to be worn by all ships, whether merchantmen or in Her Majesty's service; and, finally, this red ensign, with the new Union Jack in the upper corner, was to take the place of and be worn *instead* of the separate national Jacks previously used in the merchant ships of the subjects of the sovereign, and no other ensign was to be worn.

Here, then, ended the official authority of the separate crosses of St. George and St. Andrew, and began the reign of the "First Union Jack" of the kingdoms of England and Scotland. Then, too, was first raised the Union British ensign. The "*meteor flag*" of the realm, to be worn by all subjects of Britain's Queen on land or on sea, on merchant ships, or men-of-war, so that wherever the blood-red flag should fly, the world would know the nation to which its bearer belonged. In this red ensign (Pl. VI., fig. 2), the paramount flag of the nation, the new "Union Jack," was placed, a position which, although granted to the English Jack, had never been occupied by the "additional" Jack, whose term was then closed.

The proclamation and the drawing of the

flag, as here shown, are taken from the unique collection in the British Museum, London.

A very noticeable difference will be seen to exist between "our" new Jack of Queen Anne, of 1707, and the "additional" Jack of James, of 1606.

The white border surrounding the St. George's cross has been enlarged, and is no longer a mere margin or "fimbriation."

It has been objected by those versed in heraldry that this alteration is not in exact accordance with strict heraldic restrictions.

There is, however, another view which it is fair to entertain, namely, that it was intentional.

In the James I. flag the crosses were "*joyned according to a form made by our heralds,*" in the Queen Anne flag they are to be "*conjoyned in such manners as we should think fit.*" Most probably the Queen consulted her sailors, and this time the designers were not thinking so much of heraldry and ancient heraldic rules, as of making a flag, and, while combining the two crosses, of making two flags into one.

When the flag-makers broadened the white, they did it to restore to the Union flag a part of the white ground of the St. George's Jack, which had previously been entirely effaced, but which was now given a place in the "Union," in company with the blue ground of the St. Andrew's.

A confirmation of this will be found in the

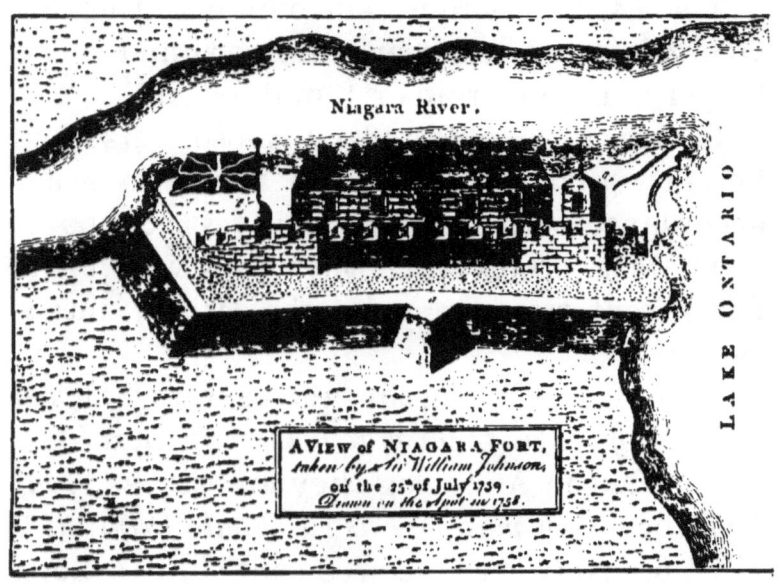

25. FORT NIAGARA, 1759.
(Reproduced from an old print.)

annals of the next change, which was made almost a century afterwards, in the Union Jack.

It may have been that some of the designers were sailors who had carried the red cross of

St. George, and now that it was being replaced in the fighting flag of the nation by the new comer, felt that it was but due to its centuries of glorious service evidence of the whole English flag, its white ground as well as its red cross, should be retained in the new national emblem.

Whether heraldically correct or not, there the broad white band first appeared, and has ever since remained, showing the red cross and white ground of St. George's Jack, combined with the white cross and blue ground of the St. Andrew's Jack, into one "Union Jack," which was thereafter to be the "sole ensign" of British rule.

It was this two-crossed Union Jack of Queen Anne which was raised at *Plassey*, when Clive won India, and at *Pondicherry* and at *Seringapatam*. Sir Wm. Johnson raisèd it above old *Fort Niagara*[*] (25) when

> "The last day came, and Bois le Grand
> Beheld with misty eyes
> The flag of France run down the staff,
> And that of England rise."
>
> —*Spina Christi.* KERBY.

---

[*]The artist would appear to have altered the flag in a sketch which he had made the previous year. An "escutcheon" will be noted in the centre of the Union.

26. THE ASSAULT AT WOLFE'S COVE, QUEBEC, 1759.
(From an old print published in London, 1760.)

Under it Wolfe stormed *Louisburg*, the key fortress of Cape Breton, and following up his victory climbed the Heights, and died victorious on the Plains of Abraham (26), when in 1759 *Quebec* was gained and Canada came under the realm of British law.

The youthful Nelson saw it fly aloft when he served as a middy on a British man-of-war, searching for the North Pole, and twenty-five years later when in glorious action he won his title as Baron Nelson of the Nile.

The *West Coast* of *Africa*, *New South Wales* and *Vancouver Island* were all added under its display, showing how the mariners of Britain were carrying it far across the distant seas, more distant than now, for those sea-dogs of the sceptred Isles had raised their new Union Jack upon the mast, and braving the unknown oceans, were sailing their ships wherever billows rolled or winds could waft them.

CHAPTER XI.

THE UNION JACK—THE EMBLEM OF PARLIAMENTARY UNION.

The kingdom of England had for centuries its own St. George's Jack and the kingdom of Scotland its cross of St. Andrew. These red and white crosses had been the accepted symbols of their separate nationalities. Each of the kingdoms had its own separate parliament, differing, it is true, from one another in methods and in many details, but representing the constitutional machinery adopted in each community for consultation between the king and his subjects who, through their representatives, advised upon matters connected with the government of their country, whether in its internal laws or in its relations with foreign powers. In course of time the same personage, in the person of James I., had by virtue of his birth succeeded to the throne of England as well as to that of Scotland. The kingly office in both the kingdoms had thus been merged in the hands of one and the same king. A new flag had been created representing the allegiance which had now been joined in the one sovereign. In this the crosses of the two kingdoms had been joined together in one design, but the separate national Jacks of each had still been retained and their use continued in force.

These separate national Jacks were certainly intended to evidence the continued separate national existence of each kingdom, while the new personal Jack or banner of the King would seem to have been intended to evidence the union of the thrones in one person, and to represent the united fealty offered to the one king. Yet it is fairly open to question as to whether this Union Jack of James I. was ever intended to mean as much as this, or whether it was not after all introduced with the purpose of avoiding trouble between the sailors of the two nations, and only intended at first to be a local convenience for the preventing of dissensions.

The new Union Jack certainly did not represent a union of the nations, else why did the two national Jacks still remain? If it had been intended to represent the fealty of his subjects to their king, why was not the red cross of the Irish included as well as the crosses of England and Scotland, for the Irish were equally subjects of James I.?

The Irish had, in fact, been subjects of his predecessors for many centuries. In 1171, after the conquest of the island had been effected by Henry II. of England, the native princes of Ireland had owned fealty to the prince not in his capacity as king, but in evidence of his position as having become by conquest the "Lord of Ireland." The country had from very early days been governed by its own parliaments, whose meetings are recorded as having taken place as early as 1295. It was not, however, until 1522 that Ireland was raised to the rank and designation of a kingdom. In this year an Act was passed by the Parliament of Ireland declaring Henry VIII., the king of England, to be also the king of Ireland. It was by virtue of this Act that the title King of Ireland was assumed by the king. The flag of England was at this same time the single St. George's Jack, yet, although the crowns were thus formally united, the cross of St. Patrick was not added to the red cross of St. George as a Union Jack in sign of the fealty to the one sovereign.

After this, the kingdom of Ireland owed fealty to three sovereigns of England in succession Edward VI., Mary, and Elizabeth, yet under none of them were the crosses of the two national flags joined together. It was not until a Scotch king, the great-grandson of Henry VIII., became King of England, that any of the three national crosses were combined. In 1603, James I. became King of Ireland and England, as well as of Scotland, yet notwithstanding that the three sister kingdoms were thus united in allegiance under his united crown, the then separate crosses of the national Jacks of each were not united in one flag. Although James I. at his accession at once added the Irish harp to the quarterings of his royal standard, being the first time that this emblem of Ireland had been inserted in the royal arms of Great Britain, yet three years passed before he entered the red cross of St. George in the additional Union Jack which he then created. All these incidents point, evidently, to the view that the union of the crosses of St. George and St. Andrew in the new flag of 1606 was not, nor could it be, an emblem of the union of thrones, but was mainly devised, as the King's proclamation distinctly stated, for the special and local purpose of keeping the sailors of the two nations most interested in shipping at peace, and so to prevent their crews from quarrelling with one another as they sailed their ships along the shores of Great Britain.

It required something more than a mere union of allegiance to create a real Union Jack, and to entitle the national crosses of the kingdoms to be entered upon its folds.

The history of the entry of the St. Patrick's cross into the Union flag enables us to see even yet more clearly what this requirement was. It will be remembered that a change in the additional Jack of James had been made in the sixth year of the reign of Queen Anne, and that the occasion of this change was coincident with the union of the separate parliaments of England and Scotland into one British parliament.

It was so soon as this occurred, but not until then, that the flag in which the two national crosses were blended was made the sole national ensign.

It was in 1707 that this first Union Jack

27. FORT GEORGE AND THE PORT OF NEW YORK IN 1770.
(From an old print.)

was created. Queen Anne was at the time Queen of Ireland as well as Queen of England and Scotland. She had quartered the harp of Ireland in her royal standard five years previously, at the time when she had commenced her reign, yet the Queen when forming her new flag did not join the cross of St. Patrick in her Union Jack any more than had King James when forming his.

For ninety-four years longer the red cross Irish Jack continued in its separate existence. The reign of Queen Anne had come to its close, and three more sovereigns in succession had ascended the united throne of Great Britain and Ireland, yet in all these reigns the Union Jack, in the red ensign, which had been declared to be the only flag of the realm to be worn by their subjects, contained only the crosses of St. George and of St. Andrew, representing but two of the kingdoms included under its rule (27).

At last, in 1801, during the forty-first year of the reign of George III., the Irish parliament was united with the Union parliament of England and Scotland, and then, and not till then, was the red cross of St. Patrick blended with the other two national crosses.

The emblem of Scotland had not been blended with that of England in one Union Jack until their parliaments had been united, so the emblem of Ireland was not added to the other two until her parliament had also been joined with theirs. So soon, then, as the three kingdoms were joined in union under one parliament, then for the first time the three crosses of the three national Jacks were united in one Union Jack. We thus have learned what was the necessary qualification to entitle a national cross to be entered in the union ensign.

It needed a union of parliaments to create a real Union Jack, one in which the three national crosses should each continue to retain their national significance and be still accorded the same precedence, when joined together in union, which had previously attached to each when separately displayed.

The history of these successive blendings shows most plainly that the triune flag arose not from union under one sovereign, but from legislative union under one parliament. The Union Jack therefore has become the emblem of the British Constitution. It is the signal of the existence of Government under British parliamentary Union, and therefore, wherever it is displayed, indicates the presence of British rule and British law.

CHAPTER XII.

THE UNION JACK AND PARLIAMENTARY UNION IN CANADA.

In addition to its harmony with the story of union in the Motherland, this Union Jack has also a most interesting connection with the extension of the powers and advantages of the British Constitution to Canada, and particularly with the establishment of responsible parliamentary government among its people.

In 1759, the seeds of the new nationality had been sown upon the Plains of Abraham, where the blood of Wolfe and Montcalm had mingled to enrich the soil.

The French forefathers of the new subjects had come very largely from those very portions of old France whose people had crossed over to England with William the Conqueror and given the British their king.

As says one of our French-Canadian historians :

"The immigration of the French, extending from 1634 to 1720, was almost entirely from among the Normans of Dieppe and Rouen, so that the settled portion of Canada was to all intents and purposes a reproduction of a Norman province. The subsequent settlers were mainly selected in Rochelle, Poictou, Paris and Normandy, to the exclusion of persons from the south and east, and coming out single, they married the daughters of the settled Normans. This accounts for the marked absence of any but the Norman accent and form of speech throughout the French-speaking communities of Canada at the present day."*

Thus the new French-speaking subjects in Canada were only returning in allegiance to the sovereignty of a king whose ancestors had been placed upon his English throne by their Norman forefathers; upon whose royal arms (28) were displayed three *fleur-de-lis* as sign of his claim, through his ancestors, to the throne of France; upon whose crown was the motto in French "Dieu et Mon Droit,"† and who by

---
* Benjamin Sulte, "The Origin of the French-Canadians."
† First used at Gisors, in Normandy, in 1198.

the retention of old customs still gave his consent to the laws enacted in his British parliament in the same old Norman phrase, "Le Roi le veult" ("The King wills it"), which had been used by his Norman forefathers.*

The French *Habitant* felt how easy was the renewal of that old relationship, and accepted the change in the way so well expressed in his Canadian voyageur patois.

28. Royal Arms of George II.

> "An' dat was de way we feel, w'en de ole *regime's* no more,
> An' de new wan come, but don't change moche;
> w'y its jus' lak' it be before,
> Spikin' *Francais* lak' we alway do, an' de English dey mak' no fuss,
> An' our law de sam', wall, I don't know me, 'twas better mebbe for us."
>
> —"*The Habitant*," W. H. Drummond.

There now commenced on this continent an evolution of internal government of the

---

* The custom is still continued, and the consent of Queen Victoria to Acts passed by Parliament is given in Norman French, "La Reine le veult."

people similar to that which had taken place in the old land of England, but under reversed conditions. An eminent French authority* has stated his belief that England owed her liberties to her having been conquered by the Normans, and to this we may add the statement of a no less important English author,† that "assuredly England was gainer by the conquest." As the advent of Norman rule to England had resulted in such privileges to the English people, so assuredly the cession of Quebec and the introduction of English government into Canada brought equal blessings to the descendants of those self-same Normans.

The French-Canadian found that under the Union Jack his property was secure. Under the *old regime* the French-Canadian had practically no voice in the government of his country. There was no elective municipal government, no freedom for public meetings, all the legislative and executive power, even to its extremest details, being centralized through the Governor and Intendant in the person of the king of France, who was two thousand miles away. Finding his religious faith untrammelled, his freedom unimpaired,

---

* Guizot, "Essais sur l'Histoire de France."   † Gibbon.

his language preserved, he soon settled down without objection, to his new sovereignty.

In 1774, the British parliament passed the Act known as the "Quebec Act," which granted an increased share of local government to the people of the great Province comprising Canada which was then set apart, and the greater portion of which is now within the present Dominion. This measure of self-government still further assured the French-descended Canadians of the protection of their liberties, so that when the English-descended colonists of the thirteen English state colonies to the south of them, revolted from their allegiance in 1775, Canada stood firm by the British crown. The descendants of the Normans were true to the form of government which their forefathers had helped to create.

The granting of separation to the thirteen United States in 1783, was followed by the immigration to Canada of those loyal souls whose hearts revolted at the action of their colonies in taking down the Union Jack, and who refused to separate themselves from the United Empire, in whose ultimate justice they had unwavering faith.

These "United Empire Loyalists" settled mainly in the western parts of Canada. Of the quarter of a million souls who then formed the total population, about a hundred and forty thousand were of French language and descent, living in the countries adjacent to the St. Lawrence River, and of the forty to fifty thousand Loyalists who, it is estimated, reached Canada during or immediately after the rebellion, over twenty-five thousand had, by 1786, settled along the Western lakes.

Government in Canada had hitherto been conducted by a Governor and a Legislative Council appointed by the Crown. A further advance in constitutional self-government was now considered desirable, and the Act of 1791 was passed. The ancient Province of Quebec was divided into two provinces, called Lower and Upper Canada, very fairly representing the localities occupied, the one by the older or French-speaking subjects of His Majesty, and the other by the new coming English-speaking loyalists, who were following their flag into the forests of the north-land.

This "Constitutional Act of 1791" gave the right of parliamentary government to the people of Canada. A Legislative Council and a House of Assembly were created for each province, the members of the latter House being elected by the people in the counties and towns of each.

The Legislature of Upper Canada held its first session at Newark (now Niagara-on-the-Lake) in 1792, summoned, as said Governor Simcoe in his opening speech, "Under the authority of an Act of Parliament of Great Britain, passed in the last year, which has established the British Constitution in this distant country." To this he added:

"The wisdom and beneficence of our Most Gracious Sovereign and the British parliament have been eminently proved not only in imparting to us the same form of government, but in securing the benefit of the many provisions which guard this memorable Act, so that the blessings of our invulnerable Constitution, we hope, will be extended to the remotest posterity."

As a sign of this self-government under the Crown, the King issued his warrant from the Court of St. James on March 4th, 1792, authorizing a "*Great Seal for the Province of Upper Canada*" (29), to be used in sealing all public

29. The Great Seal of Upper Canada, 1792.

instruments. The plate shows the details of the parts being, as described in the Royal warrant, "an anchor and a sword crossed on a calumet of peace, encircled by a wreath of olives, surmounted by an Imperial crown and the Union of Great Britain."

This "Union," which will be seen in the upper right-hand corner of the seal, was the Union Jack of Queen Anne. In drawings of the arms of the Province of Ontario (the new name given to the Province of Upper Canada at the time of Confederation, in 1867), the Jack is frequently shown as containing three crosses. A reference to the impressions made by the seal itself upon the huge pieces of white wax, four and a half inches broad by three-quarters of an inch in thickness, which have been attached by bands of parchment or of red tape to official documents, show that the "Union" contained two crosses only, namely, the cross of St. George and the single cross of St. Andrew.

The United Empire Loyalists sought their loved two-crossed Union Jack in Canada. They found it not only flying on the flagstaff, but also impressed on the seals of the grants of land which were made to them in recognition of their loyalty. On these it came to them as a sign of the surety of their legal rights under British law and their full protection under the administration of British justice.

The introduction of this Union Jack had been the result of an Act passed by the British Parliament, that mother of parliaments, which continues to this day to have vested in it the ultimate political sovereignty of every local parliament which it has created.

This Union Jack on the great seal is thus the emblem of parliamentary union between Great Britain and Canada, and the sign of the spread of the British constitutional government to the continent of America.

But the French-Canadian had also an interest in this same *Great Seal*, for on its obverse side it bore the royal coat-of-arms of the reigning sovereign, George III., and in this were still shown the three lilies of France, in the same way as in the arms of his predecessor George II. (28). What the Union Jack on the one side was to the English-speaking Canadian, the fleur-de-lis on the other, was to the French-Canadian a visible sign of his own personal connection with the glories of his forefathers, and the evidence of his glad allegiance to the sovereign who was represented by them.

This Union Jack was also shown in the arms of the Department of Education of Upper

Canada, from 1844 to 1876, during the *regime* of Dr. Ryerson as Superintendent. In these the design was the same as on the great seal, but the Union Jack was removed from the upper corner and placed upon a shield in the centre, upon which the two crosses of Queen Anne are plainly shown.*

A further adoption of the national emblem

30. UPPER CANADA PENNY.

is shown in the design on the early currency, which was coined for use in the province. The " penny " of the Bank of Upper Canada (30) shows on the one side St. George and the dragon, and, on the other, the arms of

---

* In the earlier stained glass windows placed in the Normal School, Toronto, the head offices of the Department of Education of Ontario, the three-crossed flag had been shown, but this, on the suggestion of the writer, has been corrected in the new windows placed in the library in 1896.

the great seal, having on it the Union Jack.* These were two good national emblems which, no doubt, made the money that he earned acceptable to the Canadian Loyalist, for on the coins with which he was paid for his daily labour, and on the seal of the deed of the grant of land which his Loyalist father had received for his new home, there was the imprint of the Union Jack, placed there by the Act of the Union Parliament of Great Britain, as the sign of his parliamentary union with that United Empire which commanded his allegiance.

* The design of this Bank of Upper Canada penny was made by F. W. Cumberland, the father of the writer.

CHAPTER XIII.

THE IRISH JACK.

The lineage of the Irish Jack is not so clearly defined as is that of the other Jacks. Although "Paddy" has always been so ready for a shindy, that fighting has come to be considered his "natural divarsion," he has never been considered particularly fond of the water. It is on land that he has found play for his fierce delight in mingling where the fray is thickest. It is as a soldier that the Irishman has always excelled. Wellington and Wolseley attest his power in command, and in many a forlorn hope the wild energy of the Irish blood has scaled the breach and carried the stormers past the anxious moments of the attack, displaying that same "eager, fierce, impetuous valour" with which, in the charge of the Heavy Brigade at Balaclava, "the

Inniskillings went into the massive Russian column with a cheer."*

31. St. Patrick.

It may be, as Ireland was at no time distinguished as a maritime nation, and its local shipping therefore not developed to any great extent, that the display of her national Jack was not so much in evidence among the sailors of the early days as were the Jacks of the two sister nations.

The banner of St. Patrick (31) is a white flag, having on it a cross of the same saltire shape as St. Andrew's cross, but red in colour, the heraldic description being, "*Argent, a saltire gules*," a red saltire cross on a white ground (Pl. vi., fig. 3).

St. Patrick was the apostle of the Irish, and thus became their traditional patron saint. The story of his life is that he was born in Scotland, at Kilpatrick, near Dunbarton on the Clyde, and being taken prisoner by pirates when a child, was carried into Ireland and sold there as a slave. Having acquired the native language, he escaped to the continent, and

---

* Kinglake, " Invasion of the Crimea."

afterwards becoming a Christian, and having been ordained to service in the church, returned to Ireland for the purpose of converting the people. The British name said to have been given him in his youth was *Succeath*, "valiant in war," a temperament which he certainly impressed upon the Irish, although he does not seem to have been quite so successful in transmitting his own power of refraining from hitting back. This name was afterwards, when he returned to Ireland, changed to *Patricius*, in evidence of his noble family descent, and to add importance to his mission.*

The legends of the saint date back to A.D. 411, when he is reported to have commenced his mission, and to have afterwards devoted his life to the increase of the wellbeing of the people and the spread of Christianity throughout Ireland. The tradition is that the saint suffered martyrdom upon a cross of the shape of this red cross, and thus, when he became the patron saint of Ireland, it was held in recognition as his emblem, and for that reason was adopted as the Irish cross.

Another emblem of Ireland, the green

---

* Smith's "Religion of Ancient Britain."

shamrock, is also connected in legend with St. Patrick, as having been used by him, through the lesson of its three leaves joined in one, in explaining the doctrine of the Trinity, and thus both the shamrock and the red saltire cross form the salient features of the insignia of the "Most Illustrious Order of St. Patrick," the Irish order of knighthood.

32. Labarum of Constantine.

On the other hand, some people declare that St. Patrick never had a cross, and that the cross of the saltire shape is sacred only to St. Andrew.

The Irish saltire, and also that of St. Andrew, are derived, they suggest, from the Labarum (32), or Sacred Standard, which was raised by Constantine the Great, the first Christian emperor of Rome, as the imperial standard of his armies. On this he had placed a monogram composed of the first two greek letters X R ($X\rho\iota\sigma\tau os$) of the sacred name of Christ, and the saltire cross is reputed to be the repetition of the X of the Christian emblem.

The Labarum was the official banner of the

emperor of Rome, upon it were embroidered, or set out, the insignia of the emperor of the day. These Constantine, on his conversion, had changed to the Christian emblem.

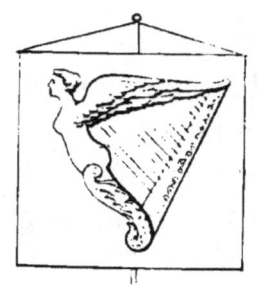

33. HARP OF HIBERNIA.

Should this latter suggestion of the origin of the cross of the saltire shape be accepted as the preferable, the saltire cross has yet a still more interesting and particular connection with the early history of Ireland.

Constantius Chlorus, the father of Constantine the Great, was the Roman governor of Britain in the reign of the Emperor Diocletian, and had, about A.D. 301, completed the pacification of Ibernia, as Ireland was then called. The pagan goddess of the island was the goddess Hibernia,* and the harp was her emblem. This Hibernian Irish harp (33) Constantius adopted as his insignia. After the resignation of Diocletian, Constantius Chlorus and Galerius were created joint emperors of Rome, and dividing the Empire

---

* Surely! Did the English add their h's in those early, as well as in later days?

between them, Galerius took the East and Constantius the West.

The death of Constantius occurred soon afterwards in England, at the city of York (Eboracum), and there he was succeeded as emperor of Rome by his son Constantine.

The persecution of the Christians in Britain, which had raged under Diocletian, and during which Alban the first British martyr had met his death at Verulam, now called St. Albans, had been in some degree restrained by Constantius, but was now completely suppressed by the new emperor. Carrying with him the germs of Christianity which he had learned in Britain, Constantine removed to the continent to engage in the contest for the command of of his Empire, and in the battle of the Milvian Bridge near Rome, in A.D. 312, he defeated Maxentius, and entered into undisputed possession of the throne. It was just before this engagement that Constantine is reported to have seen a cross shining in the heavens at midday, having on it the inscription ENTOITONIKA ("In this conquer," Latin, "*In hoc signo vinces,*") and, therefore, he adopted the Christian cross as his standard and placed the sacred monogram upon his Labarum. This victory resulted in the official recognition of the Christian religion, and the attaching to it of all the political power of the emperor of Rome.

Constantius had lived, and Constantine the Great had been brought up, in that part of England which, during the Roman occupation had been converted by the old northern country from which St. Patrick afterwards also came, and as it was to Constantine that they owed their rescue from persecution, his insignia would, therefore, be heartily received. It is very possible that the early Christianity of Ireland may, through this source, have adopted the X, the lower part of Constantine's Christian monogram, as their emblem, and in its single cross form it had become associated with the Christian labours of their apostle and patron saint. In this "story of the Irish Jack" it is a happy conception that the Labarum of Constantine the son should have given origin to the form of the Christian red cross of Ireland in return for the former emblem received from the island by his father.

Whichever may have been the source of its origin, the saltire cross is by both lines of descent intimately associated with the history of Ireland, and is rightfully claimed as its national emblem.

The origin of the Irish harp, on a blue ground, displayed in the royal standard of Great Britain, has also an ancient story, although much more modern than that of St. Patrick's cross. The arms of Ireland, before the time of Henry VII. of England (1485-1509), had consisted of three golden crowns set upon a blue ground. These ancient arms of Ireland are now worn on the helmet plate and glengarry of the Royal Munster Fusileers regiment of the British army.

Henry VIII. was the first English king who used an Irish emblem. When he was proclaimed king of Ireland, he placed the harp of Hibernia upon the coinage which he then issued, but he did not introduce either the harp or the red cross of St. Patrick into his royal arms, nor upon his banners.

The first English sovereign to use an Irish emblem in the official insignia was Queen Elizabeth, who introduced one in the design of her "great seal." Instead of using the three Irish crowns, she inserted a harp as the emblem of the nation. James I., her successor, was the first king to introduce an Irish emblem into the royal standard, and ever since then the golden harp of Hibernia, on the ancient blue ground of the three Irish crowns, has been shown in one of the quarters of the British standard as the emblem of Ireland. In the arms of all the sovereigns, from James I., 1603, to and including William IV., 1837, the front of the harp was formed by a female figure, intended most probably to represent the goddess Hibernia. During the early Victorian period a change has been been introduced in the shape of the harp, which has been altered to that of the ancient Irish harp, connected in form and in legend with King Brian Boru (Boroimhe).

The exploits of this most noted of the early kings of Ireland had been mainly devoted to the defence of his kingdom against the invasions of the Danes during the period when, under Canute, they had well nigh conquered all England.

Although in the main successful, he was slain in battle with them, according to some, in 1039,[*] or, as others report, in the hour of victory over the Danes, at Clontarf, near Dublin, in 1014.[†]

That the king had accepted Christianity is

---

[*] King, "National Arms."
[†] "Haydn's Index."

is attested by his having, in 1004, presented a golden votive offering upon the altar of the church at Armagh, and here, in accordance with his dying request, his body was buried after the battle of Clontarf.*

This city of Armagh is reputed to have been founded about A.D. 445, by St. Patrick, and to this account is accredited the ecclesiastical pre-eminence which has always enshrined the city, for the Bishop of Armagh is the "Archbishop and Primate of all Ireland" of the Protestant Church, and it is the see city also of the Primate of Ireland of the Roman Catholics.

The minstrelsy of the Irish harper has held sway and been cherished through all the ages by the Irish people, whose temperament may have been affected, or else has been most touchingly expressed by its strange and mystic cadences. The sweet pathos of these ancient melodies has given tone and inspiration to most of the Irish songs, markedly to those of the sweet singer Moore, whose music has installed in affectionate memory

"The harp that once through Tara's halls
The soul of music shed."

---

* "Ulster Journal of Archæology," Vol. I., September, 1804.

Of all the traditional patrons of music, King Brian Boru was the most renowned, and thus in poetry and song his name became identified with the Irish harp. In the old seal of Carrickfergus (34), granted by James I., the form of this ancient harp of Brian Boru is excellently displayed. Around the margin is the Latin inscription:

34. SEAL OF CARRICKFERGUS, 1605.

"SIGILL . CVSTVM . PORTVS . CARIGFERGI . ANO,"

within the circles are the initials of the King, I. R. (James Rex), and the date, 1605, and on the shield in the centre are three Irish harps, having the rounded front pillar and the curious upper sweep of the neck, termed the harmonic curve, of the type known as that of Brian Boru.

Although this Irish harp was introduced in the seal of the Irish city during his reign, the emblem placed in his royal arms by James I. as the emblem of Ireland was the angelic harp of Hibernia, and in this shape it remained on the royal standards of all the succeeding sovereigns until Queen Victoria, in whose arms (35), and on whose banner, it is frequently displayed.

As the pagan emblem had, through the banner of Constantine, been changed to the Christian cross of St. Patrick, so now centuries afterwards, the Hibernian harp in the royal standard was changed to the Irish harp of the Christian king, Brian Boru, and through the grave at Armagh again connected with Ireland's patron saint. Thus, whether it be cross or harp, the emblems of Ireland are associated with St. Patrick.

35. ARMS OF QUEEN VICTORIA.

During one period in the story of our flag, Ireland had been represented on its folds, as shown in Cromwell's Jack, and in the Commonwealth ensign, but it was not by a cross, as were the other nationalities, but by the gold harp of Hibernia upon a blue ground.

The Irish red cross on a white ground had been the banner of the Fitzpatricks at the time of the conquest of Ireland under Henry II., and it still appears in the arms of their family; but does not seem to have been formally recognized as the general national emblem for Ireland until about the close of the seventeenth century.

Though the kings of England had, since Henry II., in 1771, been "lords paramount," and since Henry VIII. been "kings of Ireland," the national Jack of Ireland had not been joined with the other Jacks. When the crosses of St. George and St. Andrew were combined in the "additional Jack" of James, in 1606, it was not included, nor was it afterwards in the first Union Jack of Queen Anne, in 1707; so that for all these centuries the red cross of St. Patrick had continued alone. At length, the time had come when another change was to be made in the Union Jack, and in 1801, under George III., the red saltire cross first joined the two sister crosses. For the immediately previous two hundred years the Irishman had gallantly contributed his prowess to the glories won under the two-crossed Jack, in which his nation was not represented; but from this time onward his own Irish cross entered into its proper place in the national Jack, and received its acknowledged share as the emblem of his kingdom.

CHAPTER XIV.

THE JACK OF GEORGE III.—1801.

THE SECOND AND PRESENT UNION JACK.

We come now to the formation of the three-crossed Jack, the "Red, white and blue" of story and of song, being the second Union Jack (36).

In the forty-first year of the reign of George III. the three kingdoms had been brought into complete union, whereupon proclamation was issued by the king, of which the following extracts are given :

EXTRACTS.

From a Proclamation by the King dated St. James' Palace, January 1st, 1801.

Declaring His Majesty's pleasure concerning the royal style and titles appertaining to the Imperial crown of the united kingdom of Great Britain and Ireland and its dependencies, and also the ensigns armorial, flags and banners thereof.

> . . . "And that the arms or ensigns armorial of the said United Kingdoms shall be quarterly; first and fourth England, second Scotland, third Ireland, and it is our will and pleasure that there shall be borne therewith on an escutcheon of pretence the arms of our Dominions in Germany."

The result of this clause was that the lilies of France, which had been quartered in the royal arms since Edward III., 1327, were altogether removed, and the whole four quarters were appropriated, two quarters to the three golden lions of England, and one quarter each to the red lion of Scotland and the golden harp of Ireland, and upon a small shield on the centre was to be placed the white horse of Hanover, to indicate the other country over which the king also reigned.

36. Union Jack of George III., 1801.

... "And it is our will and pleasure that the standard of the said united kingdoms shall be the same quarterings as are hereinbefore declared to be the arms or ensigns armorial of the said united kingdoms." ...

The royal standard is ordered to have in it only the arms of the three united kingdoms of England, Scotland and Ireland.

"And that the union flag shall be *azure, the crosses saltires of St. Andrew and St. Patrick, quarterly per saltire counterchanged, argent and gules; the latter fimbriated of the second, surmounted by the cross of St. George of the third, fimbriated as the saltire.*"

In making the Union Jack, the instructions were that the white cross of Scotland and the red cross of Ireland were to be joined together quarterly and "counterchanged," and that the red cross of St. George was to "surmount," that is, to be laid upon the surface of them both.

The designers of this new Union Jack of 1801 had this time to join three flags together, instead of as in 1707 only joining two. The problem set before them being the union of the three national Jacks of the sister nations into one grand Union Jack (Pl. vii., fig. 1).

The construction of the new flag presents some important details, which teach some very interesting lessons. The construction was in the hands of the flag-makers, and the regulations for the making of the new flag

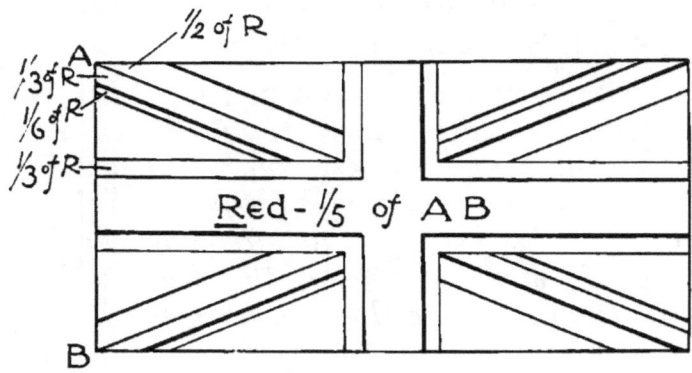

37. Outline Jack. The Proper Proportions of the Crosses.

were issued at the same time as the proclamation, and are the same as those of our Admiralty regulations of the present day.

From these directions, it is clearly evident that the recognition which the white ground of St. George's Jack had been given in the flag of 1707 was intended to be continued, and a striking confirmation is given of the correctness of the suggestion which was offered as being the reason for that broadening of the white border to the red cross of St. George which had occurred in the making of the Union Jack of Queen Anne.

An outline drawing (37) of the flag is given for convenience of comparison. The proportions of the several crosses and borders are directed to be made as follows, the measurement of the "width of the flag" being the measurement on the "halliard" or "hoist," being the side next to the flagstaff:

Red cross of St. George, - $\frac{1}{5}$ of width of the flag.
White border to St. George, $\frac{1}{3}$ of red of St. George.
Red cross of St. Patrick, - $\frac{1}{3}$ " " "
White border to St. Patrick, $\frac{1}{6}$ " " "
Broad White of St. Andrew, $\frac{1}{2}$ " " "

The paramount cross of St. George is made the factor by which the measurements of all the other parts are to be regulated, and its own width is to be one-fifth of the width of the flag on the flagstaff.

The crosses of the other two Jacks, to be joined, are each allotted a proportion of one-third the width of the cross of St. George. The divisions of the parts for the Irish Jack

PRESENT UNION JACK

JACK WRONGLY MADE

JACK WRONGLY PLACED.

are stated separately as *one-third* for the red cross of St. Patrick, and *one-sixth* for its white border, the two measurements, when added together, amounting to a proportion of *one-half*.

The proportion of *one-half* allotted to the "broad white of St. Andrew," comprises the due share of *one-third* for the Scotch cross, and *one-sixth* for its border, being an exact equality to the proportions given to the Irish cross and its border.

The measurements of the "cross" and its "border" of the Scotch Jack are stated in one figure, because their colours are the same, while those of the Irish Jack are given separately, because the colours are different, the cross being red and its border white.

The national banners of St. Patrick and St. Andrew are thus given each a proportion of *one-third* for each cross, and *one-sixth* for its border or "fimbriation."

In complying with the instruction of the blazon respecting the red cross of St. George, that it should be "fimbriated as the Saltire," that is, for what in other words is stated "for the white border to the cross of St. George" there is allotted, not simply the one-sixth proportion due to a "*fimbriation*," but the full proportion of one-third, equivalent to that of a *national cross*.

The width of the border cannot this time be said to be the result of the "carelessness of a draughtsman,"* for it is made with premeditated carefulness, and more than that, the measurements are set down in exact figures.

Thus the surmise for the broadening of the border in the flag of 1707 has been amplified in the flag of 1801, as this broad white border, given to surround the red cross of St. George, and now clearly established in its equality of representation with a national cross, is not only the formal recognition of the white ground of the English Jack, which had been restored to the flag in 1707, but is also a recognition of the white ground of the Irish Jack, which was now for the first time entering the Union Jack.

In this Union Jack of 1801, we have then plainly displayed a complete representation of the three separate crosses and of the white and blue grounds of the three national Jacks

---

* MacGeorge, "Flags."

which were then combined together to form the Union Jack.

No participation in this division of the space may, however, be attributed to the "Officers of Arms" of the day, for it has been expressly put on record that "*in this allotment they were not allowed the exercise of their own judgment,*" and that in their opinion the "*science of heraldry has been set at defiance.*"*

In fact, ever since this flag first appeared, there have been perrenial uprisings of heraldic bile and many learned arguments about the correct interpretation to be given to the "blazon," and in the explanation of the wording "*fimbriated as the saltire.*" The person who made the drawings of the first flag has been termed "either careless, or ignorant, or stupid, most probably all three."

To one objector, during this present reign, answer was officially returned by Garter King of Arms, that "The flag was made according to the drawing, and it was exhibited in the same way on the colours of the Queen's infantry regiments." There was, in fact, noth-

---

* *Naval and Military Magazine*, 1827, p. 182.

ing more to be said, and thus both on sea and on land all the official flags are made in the same way. There is no doubt that the flag-makers whose minds were occupied in joining three *flags* were not at the time much hampered by the niceties of armorial restrictions or æsthetic traditions. If the heralds are not exactly satisfied with the way the divisions were made, due honour has at least been done to each of the Jacks of the three kingdoms, while at the same time the historical value of the " Union " is greatly enhanced and its beauty as a flag most certainly increased.

In the heraldic and traditional interpretation of colours, red indicates courage, white is the emblem of purity, and blue the emblem of truth.

By this better and more equal division of the colours in the flag much additional emphasis is given to the story which those colours tell :

> " Red, white and blue.
> Brave, pure and true."

Lessons which, as well as the other lessons which it bears, should be deeply impressed upon the minds of our children, so that they may endeavour to live lives worthy of the ideals of their national flag, and frame the character of their nation by its teachings.

Since 1801, no change has been made in this Union Jack of George III., which was the second of its race, and is, in 1897, our present Union Jack.

CHAPTER XV.

THE LESSONS OF THE CROSSES.

The combinations of the Jacks have at length been completed, and the three crosses been placed together in the one flag of 1801.

That it is a beautiful and easily distinguished flag is admitted on all hands, but it has a still further quality of immeasurable value in a national flag, that its parts and colours tell the history of the nation whose emblem it is. To those who know the story of the three separate national flags, the Union Jack, with its three crosses, its white borders and eight blue triangles, tells how the present Empire has been formed upon the three kingdoms which were combined to make it. Laid broadly upon the whole combination, and "surmounting" it, and also forming the basis for all its measurements, is the plain red cross of St. George, indicating in such a way that the simplest mind can understand the predominant share which the English nation has borne in the creation of the union, and the powerful position which it holds in its councils.

Under this cross, and supporting it, are the white and red crosses of the two junior nations, which are themselves, in their turn, supported on the white and blue grounds, which form the basis foundations of the flag.

Thus clearly does the position of the crosses teach the lesson of how England had taken the leading part among the three sister nations in the creation of their British Empire, and how, supporting each other, they all are united by *courage* to build their Realm on the sure foundations of *purity* and *truth*.

But there is another lesson of the relations between the Scotch and Irish nations themselves, which the crosses also plainly tell.

The flag is divided by the cross of St. George into four quarters, in all of which the saltire crosses of St. Andrew and St. Patrick are, as the heraldic *blazon* of the proclamation says, "quarterly per saltire counterchanged."

Fierce and endless have been the discussions between heraldic experts as to whether the word in the blazon should be "counter-charged" or "counterchanged." The latter is the word given in this proclamation, and although the flag may, in the opinion of some of the heralds, be an "extraordinary amalgamation"* and the blazon "not only very obscure but a positive jumble of terms" † yet the intention of the designers has been carried out in the flag itself.

The cross of Scotland occupies the higher position in the first and third quarters, and the cross of Ireland in the second and fourth. The relative positions of the Irish and Scotch crosses, as they are placed in the first and second quarters, which are next the flagstaff, are reversed in the third and fourth quarters, which are the quarters at the end of the flag.

It will be noted (36) that, in the first and second quarters, the broad white of the cross of St. Andrew is placed above and the red cross and its border are beneath; while in the third and fourth quarters, the red cross of St. Patrick and its border are above, and the broad white is underneath.

That is to say, the positions of the crosses

---

* *Gentleman's Magazine*, January, 1801.
† *Naval and Mil'tary Magazine*, March, 1827.

are alternately changed about, or "counterchanged."

The quarters of the flag next the flagstaff are considered to be of higher importance than the others, and in these more important quarters the cross of St. Andrew is given precedence over the cross of St. Patrick.

The lesson intended to be taught by the position of the crosses is plain. The kingdom of Scotland had entered into the union with England before the kingdom of Ireland, and, therefore, the white cross of St. Andrew is given the precedence over the red cross of St. Patrick.

These important and intentional divisions of the space in the flag were plainly devised, but unfortunately are often omitted to be followed.

Flags are sometimes to be seen (Pl. VII., fig. 2) in which the white border around the red cross of St. George is reduced to the same narrow size as the border of St. Patrick, and thus the white grounds of the Jacks of England and Ireland are displaced.

Still more often the red cross of St. Patrick is set full in the centre of the transverse cross, and thus the cross of St. Andrew is completely expunged, for its white is reduced to only two narrow white margins in equal size on both sides of the Irish red cross. The broad white of St. Andrew has thus been entirely lost.

Sufficient care, too, is not taken in setting the flag upon the flagstaff. When the red ensign, or any similarly quartered flag, is reversed on the flagstaff, that is to say, displayed with the Union down, it becomes a signal of distress. Union Jacks are often seen hoisted upside down (Pl. VII., fig. 3). No more distressful act can be done to the Union Jack than to reverse its crosses by putting the wrong end next the staff, with the broad white saltire down; nor greater indignity be done to its people than by destroying the position of their national Jacks.

Such errors cannot be too greatly lamented, or be too carefully avoided, for by them dishonour is done to the memory of the nations whose prowess has ennobled their national emblems, and the beautiful "Story of the Union Jack" is utterly marred, for the positions of the crosses and the borders cease to tell the consecutive history of the Empire nation whose combined union emblem they form.

From 1801 onward dates our present Union

ENGLAND EXPECTS EVERY MAN WILL DO HIS D U T Y

NELSON'S SIGNAL.

Jack, in which all three nations are represented. It was born when the power of Great Britain seemed to be almost wrecked. Reverses had accumulated upon her. In America, thirteen of her longest established and most populous colonies had revolted from her sway, and foresworn their allegiance. In Europe, the nations of France, Spain and Holland were united in arms against her, and she was battling almost single-handed against the power of the great Napoleon; yet, undaunted by these trials, the sons of the united nations ran their new Union Jack up aloft, and started out to frame that marvellous career which it has since achieved.

This second Union Jack rejoiced at Aboukir in 1802, when Abercrombie crushed Napoleon out of Egypt; with it were won the triumphs of Wellington, from Assaye in India, through Badajoz and Spain, to the crowning victory at Waterloo. It was the flag which floated in the "white ensign" on all the ships at Trafalgar, and on the main topgallant head of the *Victory** when Nelson sent aloft his British watchword:

"England expects every man will do his duty."
—(Pl. I. fig. 1).

---

* As the flagship of the Admiral of the fleet.

The halo of that watchword shone around it at Balaclava, when the heroes of the valley charge proved it was

> "Theirs not to reason why,
> Theirs not to make reply,
> Theirs but to do and die."

And again at sea, above the *Birkenhead*, when five hundred steadfast men went down beneath its folds, inspired by its duty call.

In Africa, at Isandula, Melville and Coghill wrapped it around their bodies and won death to save it from the foe; and for it the forty mounted riflemen of Matabeleland died in their tracks, singing, "God save the Queen"; and on this continent of America the impetuous Brock, facing enormous odds, gave up his life for it on the cedar-clad slopes of Queenston Heights, and beneath it the French-Canadians of Beauharnois knelt on the battle-field, and, rising, won with De Salaberry and his Voltigeurs the victory of glorious Chateauguay.*

---

* Captain Langtin caused his men of the Beauharnois Militia to kneel, went through a short prayer with them, and then, rising, said, "Now that they had fulfilled their duty to their God, they would fulfil that to their King."—LIGHTALL, "*The Battle of Chateauguay.*"

If those crosses could but speak, what glories they could tell! and yet the outlines of the flag, when they are properly displayed, signal the story of the crosses as plainly and as eloquently as if they told it in burning words.

CHAPTER XVI.

THE UNION JACK, THE FLAG OF CANADA.

UNDER THE TWO CROSSES.

ALTHOUGH the Union Jack has been constructed from the local Jacks of the three island kingdoms, its greatest glories have been won in expeditions sent across the seas to other lands. The natives of the parent isles have never needed to raise it as their signal in driving invaders from their shores, and in this way it does not bear to them that added vitality which it bears to the resident Canadian, of being associated with brave defence of home and native land. To the Englishman, Irishman or Scotchman, in his own island home, it is the emblem of foreign conquest; to the emigrant or the Canadian born, it is much more, as being the patriot signal of national defence.

After the contest of 1759, Canada had settled down into the paths of peace, soldier and *habitant* had vied in binding up one another's wounds, and evidencing all the pleasantries of reconciliation.*

A memorial, the like of which has never been known elsewhere, either in history or the world, has been erected in the square of Quebec to the two heroes, Montcalm and Wolfe, equal in valour, equal in fame. An united sentiment raised this single monument to their united memory, bearing upon it the noble inscription :

MORTEM, VIRTUS, COMMUNEM.
FAMAM, HISTORIA
MONUMENTUM, POSTERITAS, DEDIT.†

As the glory of their champions was thus intertwined, so the patriotism of the old occupants and the new-comers to Canada began from this splendid beginning to blend more closely in fraternal union.

---

* The nuns of the convents of Quebec sewed together blankets to make trousers for the 78th Fraser Highlanders, who otherwise would have had no protection against the snows during the first winter of their occupation of the citadel of Quebec.

† "Valour gave them a common death, history a common fame, posterity a common monument."

The Treaty of Paris, in 1763, confirmed the Union Jack in its position of being the successor on the continent of America of the fleur-de-lis over all the territory stretching from Labrador southward, along the Atlantic coast to Florida, and inland, westward as far as the waters of the Mississippi.

In pursuance of this treaty, King George III. issued his proclamation (October, 1763,) creating four provinces and governments, named Quebec, East Florida, West Florida and Granada, this last consisting of the islands of the West Indies. Of these four provinces Quebec was the territory lying adjacent to the St. Lawrence river system, extending from the river's mouth to the head waters on the watersheds of the farthest inland lakes.

By this proclamation French Canada ceased to be a conquered country, and became a colony of the king. It was to be governed by a governor and an assembly, entitled to arrange its own taxation, having control of its own internal welfare and good government, and empowered to institute its own courts of law; but to every subject, new or old, of the king, there was reserved the right of appeal to the foot of the throne itself in the Privy Council

CANADIAN RED ENSIGN

CANADIAN BLUE ENSIGN

SUGGESTED CANADIAN ENSIGN

The Union Jack, the Flag of Canada. 177

of Great Britain, should any person think themselves aggrieved by the decision of their own locally appointed courts.*

The French-Canadian subject soon began to find for himself the beneficent character of British rule. He was no longer harried by an irresponsible Governor or a grasping Intendant for the enrichment of a foreign court, but was assisted in every way in the local development of his country. His personal property was secure, and he soon became sensible of the certainty of English law.

An Act of Parliament followed, formally and still further guaranteeing to the French-speaking subjects the quiet continuance of their most cherished customs.†

The Quebec Act of 1774 confirmed the *habitant* in the free exercise of his Roman Catholic religion, and restored to him his old French civil law, but provided that in all criminal matters the law of England which had been found so satisfactory was to remain in force. This Act was passed by the British Parliament at Westminster, and thus its powers were under the two-crossed Jack of

---
* Royal Proclamation under Treaty of Paris, 1763.
† Quebec Act, 1774, Sec. XI.

Queen Anne, the ensign of parliamentary rule, formally extended to the new world.

Content with his lot, secure in his home, and sure that good faith would ever be kept with him, the French-Canadian proved loyal to the trust confided to him.

In 1775, after having been for sixteen years an English colony, Canada was invaded by the forces of the thirteen older English colonies to the south, which had consorted together in revolution against their parent state. After entering Montreal, which had been abandoned to them, they concentrated around the ramparts of Quebec, for an assault upon the Citadel. Below were the rebels against the British crown, above upon the Queen's bastion of Cape Diamond flew the two-crossed Union Jack of Queen Anne, and within the fortress, under Sir Guy Carleton, the friend and fellow-soldier of Wolfe, was a garrison of 1,800 men, one-third of whom were French-Canadian militia, headed by Col. Lecompte Dupre. The invaders from New York were, however, reckoning without their host. They had expected to find the French-Canadians dissatisfied with their lot, and as restless as themselves, but instead, they found them standing firm side by side with their British friends, who were joined with them in common defence of their native Canadian land.

The assault commenced on the night of December 31st, 1775. At the point of attack at Pres de Ville, in lower town, the guard was under the command of Captain Chabot and Lieutenant Picard of the French-Canadian militia, and the guns were served by sailors from the British ships with Sergeant Hugh McQuarters of the Royal Artillery in charge. The attack was boldly met, General Montgomery, the leader of the United States forces was killed, General Arnold, his second in command wounded, and the whole invading force was put to rout.

Thus once again were the historic heights and walls of old Quebec crowned with a British victory, but this time with one in which the French-Canadians themselves were the brave defenders of the Union Jack.

No wonder the French-speaking Canadian looks upon this flag with pride, and as one of his compatriots, Sir Adolphe Chapleau, the present Lieutenant-Governor of Quebec, has so well said, " is French in nationality, but

British in patriotism," for beneath the Union Jack he dwells secure in possession of his dearest rights, and under it has victoriously driven the United States invaders back each time they have ventured to attack his loved Canadian soil.

While such loyalty to the national flag was shown in eastern Canada, so was it also later on in the country farther west.

The thirteen southern colonies had completed their revolution in 1783. Immediately thereafter the "coming of the Loyalists" had commenced in the districts of Nova Scotia and New Brunswick, but was principally directed to the western province of Upper Canada, all three of these provinces being now included in the Dominion or Union of Canada.

These western lands were then uninhabited, save by the native Indian tribes and a few white settlers, who had been attracted to the districts by the chances of trapping for furs or of trading with the Indians.

The gallantry of the French-speaking Britons at Quebec, in 1775, had kept the Union Jack flying above Canadian soil, and to Canada's unbroken forests in the western province these English-speaking loyalists therefore came, because there they would have their old loved flag once more continuing above them.

Never does history anywhere relate such loyalty to a flag as was shown by this migration of the U. E. Loyalists,* that men should give up homes, farms, companionship and wealth, and taking up their wives and little ones, should follow a flag for conscience' sake into an undeveloped and almost unknown land!

> "Right staunch and true to the ties of old,
>   They sacrificed their all,
> And into the wilderness set out,
>   Led on by Duty's call.
> The aged were there with their snow-white hair,
>   And their life-course nearly run,
> And the tender, laughing little ones,
>   Whose race had just begun."
>
> —*"The Lion and the Lilies,"* JAKEWAY.

It was enough for them that the Union Jack was the flag of Canada; so they followed it to the far north. Here they lived out the

---

* "United Empire Loyalists," so-called because they preferred to remain united with the parent Empire rather than become citizens of another State.

balance of their days, and, dying, have been buried in the sacred soil beneath its folds. Certain it is that their descendants will ever prove true to their loyal faith that no other realm shall possess their bones nor other nation's flag fly above their graves.

Such, then, was the esteem in which Canadians held the two-crossed Union Jack, even before this present century had commenced. In eastern Canada the French-speaking loyalist had laid down his life in its defence, and, preserved by this loyalty to the country farther west, the old English-speaking loyalist there sought his new home in the far-off forest, so that he and his loved ones might continue to live beneath its sway.

Truly was this two-crossed Union Jack the flag of Canada, and as truly is its three-crossed successor, the native and national birthright of the sons of these patriot pioneers.

CHAPTER XVII.

THE UNION JACK, THE FLAG OF CANADA.

UNDER THE THREE CROSSES.

In 1801 the "new" three cross union had entered into the upper corner of the red ensign of British rule. The Canadians, both French and English, had been faithful to its two-crossed predecessor, and now again their patriotism was to be put to the test.

The parent kingdom of Great Britain had been for nineteen years engaged in its mighty struggle with the great Napoleon for the supremacy of Europe, and the time seemed opportune to the envious people of the United States for gaining an advantage over the nation from which they had separated their allegiance, and also, though covertly, for striking a blow at the neighbouring people who had so successfully resisted their previous invasion.

The quarrel was none of Canada's making, nor one in which she had any share, and although the ostensible reason which had been alleged by the United States as cause of offence was repealed before hostilities had been commenced, yet war was declared by them on the 18th of June, 1812.*

The population of the United States at that time amounted to no less than eight millions, while in Canada, from end to end, there were but four hundred thousand souls all told.

Yet the Canadians did not quail, their country was to be the scene of war, their homes to be stake for which the nations were to strive. Aid they could not expect from their British friends across the sea, already strained to the utmost in their long conflict with the armies of Europe, their reliance must be upon their own stout hearts and strong right arms, but this was enough, for

"Odds lie not in numbers, but in spirit, too."

Only four thousand five hundred regular trained soldiers, were in Canada in 1812, and

---

* The British Orders-in-Council respecting the "right of search," to which the United States made objection, and had been given as their reason for war, had been repealed in England the day before war was declared.

in them are included men of the Newfoundland and Glengarry regiments, recruited locally in the colony, and thus the brunt of the defence was to fall upon the stalwart but untrained militia of the country-side.

The tide of invasion advanced north against Canada from the United States. For three years, from 1812 to 1815, the contest went on. Our Frenchmen again bravely took up their arms, and this time, under their new three-crossed Jack, again drove the United States' invader back, making the names of Chateauguay and Chrystler's Farm ring down through history in token of the victories which they won beneath it in defence of their Canadian liberties and homes. So, too, their English-speaking brothers of Upper Canada won equal victories for this same Union Jack. At the capitulation of Fort Detroit, in the State of Michigan, the American soldiers laid down their arms before it. At Queenston Heights, under the glorious Brock, at Stoney Creek and Beaver Dams, Niagara and Lundy's Lane, the American invader was sent in quick retreat from Canadian soil, and at the conclusion of the three years' war, after all the varying success, there was not one foot of Canada, from end to end, which was occupied or sullied by the foot of the foreign foe.

Thus all along their frontier shores, from Mackinac to far St. John, the Canadians stood shoulder to shoulder in one bold united line, and held the larger half of North America for the British crown.

. . . .

"Since when has a Southerner placed his heel
On the men of the Northern Zone?"

Shall the mothers that bore us bow the head
And blush for degenerate sons?
Are the patriot fires gone out and dead?
Ho! brothers stand to the guns!
Let the flag be nailed to the mast,
Defying the coming blast!
For Canada's sons are as true as steel,
Their metal is muscle and bone,
The Southerner never shall place his heel
On the men of the Northern Zone.

Oh, we are the men of the Northern Zone,
Where the maples their branches toss;
And the Great Bear rides in his state alone,
Afar from the Southern Cross.
Our people shall aye be free,
They never shall bend the knee,

> For this is the land of the true and leal,
> Where freedom is bred in the bone—
> The Southerner never shall place his heel
> On the men of the Northern Zone.
>
> —*The Men of the Northern Zone,*
> Kernighan (The Khan).

Again, when Fenian hordes and restless soldiers, who had been disbanded from the armies of the American civil war, were assembled and drilled under the protection of the government of the United States, and launched in raids against Canadian homes, the Canadian volunteers rallied under their Union Jack, and, in 1866, along the Niagara Frontier, and in 1870, at Eccles Hill, in the Province of Quebec, again drove the southern invader back, and held their native soil inviolate beneath its three-crossed folds.

The Union Jack was now to include another parliamentary union in the story of its career.

Up to 1867 the Eastern British Provinces in North America had remained under separate local governments, such as had been established in the previous century; but in this year Nova Scotia, New Brunswick and Upper and Lower Canada were all united in the one Dominion of Canada, then extending only as far as Lake

Superior. This "Act of Confederation" was passed in London, at Westminster, by the parliament of Great Britain, and thus the union parliament of the Union Jack was parent to the new union parliament established in United Canada. Each province continued to have its own "Provincial Assembly," in which legislation is conducted on matters pertaining to its own local or Home Rule, but all general powers are centered in the one parliament of Canada. Hitherto the spirit of the flag had been solely that of union with the Motherland, thereafter it had an added and wider meaning, for it became the symbol of Canadian union as well, the patriot flag of the new Daughter Nation which had thus been brought into existence in the outer British realm. Inspired by this union, the older provinces thus united began to extend their borders, and soon Manitoba and the Hudson Bay Territories of the central prairies were added (1869), and British Columbia joined (1871), followed by Prince Edward Island (1873), to make the one great Dominion of Canada, now stretching across the continent of America from sea to sea.

Difficulties, of course, were met in this consolidating of the territories, but the sign of

THE UNION JACK, THE FLAG OF CANADA. 189

union was flying from the flagstaff, and the new born patriotism surmounted them all. In March, 1885, when the spirit of discontent arose among the Metis of the North-West, and a rebellion broke out, the courage of the united Canadians was aroused with electric flash, and the volunteer battalions from the far Atlantic shores, from French-speaking Quebec, from the great Ontario Lakes, and from all parts of the Dominion, vied with one another in bearing the privations of forced marches across the frozen lakes, or over the pathless prairies, to reach the scene of action, and join in maintaining the supremacy of their new-born union. The rebellion was quickly suppressed; but the events at Fish Creek, Batoche, and on the banks of the Saskatchewan left gaps in the loyal ranks.

38. THE WAR MEDAL, 1793-1814.

"Not in the quiet church-yard near those who loved them best,
But by the wild Saskatchewan they laid them to their rest;
A simple soldier's funeral in that lonely spot was theirs,
Made consecrate and holy by a nation's tears and prayers,
Their requiem, the music of the rivers singing tide;
Their funeral wreaths, the wild flowers that grew on every side;
Their monument, undying praise from each Canadian heart,
That hears how, for their country's sake, they nobly bore their part."

Two medals* granted by their sovereign commemorated the gallantry of the Canadians who fought beneath the Union Jack in 1812-13, for union with the Motherland (38), and in 1885 for union within Canada itself (39).

These are some of the causes which have given rise to the stirring patriotism evinced by Canadians for their national flag, and have kept aflame the passionate fervour of their loyalty.

Four times within the century—in 1776, 1812, 1866 and 1870—has their flag been raised in defence of home and native land; and once, in 1885, for maintenance of union within themselves.

---

* See Appendix "Canadian War Medals."

As Canadians see it waving above their school-houses and over their homes, they read in its crosses the story that they tell, and remember that the deep red folds have been freshened and coloured in the heart-blood of Canada's sons, poured out on their own loved soil. The sons of the parent-nations have carried it in many a far-off strife, but in their own island homes, "*compassed by the inviolate sea,*" they sleep secure, and never have had to fight beneath it in defence of native land. It is in this regard that Canadians can cherish it even more than they who first carried it, and may now rightly wear it as their very own, for the three-crossed Union Jack is so bound up with love of country, defence of home and all that is glorious in Canada's history, that it is the flag of Canada itself.

39. THE NORTH-WEST CANADA MEDAL.

CHAPTER XVIII.

THE UNION JACK OF CANADA THE FLAG OF LIBERTY IN AMERICA.

There is something more than mere valorous devotion which should be aroused in the expression of loyalty for a flag. This devotion might be found even under a despot's sway, for the race or native sympathy of its upholders might cause sentiment, even under the most adverse conditions to overpower all sense of judgment, and reckless valour take the place of thoughtful allegiance.

The story of an ideal flag should declare a supreme idea, an idea which has been so well expressed as being the "*divine right of liberty in man. Not lawlessness, not license, but organized institutional liberty—liberty through law, and laws for liberty.*"*

When a flag records by the unmistakable

---

* Henry Ward Beecher.

story of its life, how this desired liberty has been, not simply talked about, but granted in actual fact to all who have reached the lands of its dominion, and, further, tells how the amplest dream of self-government is realized by those who dwell beneath its sway, then indeed is that flag to be cherished with the most passionate devotion and valued in the most critical estimation.

The folds of such a flag become an inspiration, not only to the heart, but to the mind, and men may well be willing to risk their all, and even life itself, for the maintenance of its unsullied honour.

Such a flag is the Union Jack of Canada.

This Jack in Canada is not only the national ensign of the British race, but it is more, for as upheld by Canadians, it has ever been the real "flag of liberty" in America.

The greatest pride of the Union Jack is that

> "Though it may sink o'er a shot-torn wreck,
> It never flies over a slave."

This fact is true of the Jack of to-day throughout all the British territories, but it has not always been so. It has been the happy lot of the Motherland, the cradle of the liberties of the earth, that freedom has been enjoyed for many centuries on her own home-soil, but even there the legal doctrine was not judicially established until 1772, when the notable decision of Lord Mansfield declared that, "on the soil of the British Isles the slave is free." The abolition of slavery under the Union Jack was not declared by statute of the British parliament until 1811; and even after that, slavery continued in the outer realms, so that in 1820 there were no fewer than 340,000 slaves under British rule in the island of Jamaica alone.

At last, in 1833, the glorious Act of Emancipation was passed by the British parliament, and the same freedom which had existed on the soil of the parent-kingdom was extended to all races who lived anywhere under the Union Jack. The people of the parent-isles then gave further proof that this was done, not solely in the pursuit of an ideal, but out of real good-will, for they not only proclaimed the blessings of freedom to the slave, but also purchased his emancipation by themselves paying $100,000,000 to his owners in those colonies in which slavery had, up to that time, existed with their consent. In the true spirit of British fair-play, they thus scouted the idea of exercising their Christianity at other people's expense.

	Number of Slaves.	Indemnity Paid.
*Jamaica	311,700	£6,152,000
Barbadoes	83,000	1,721,000
Trinidad	22,300	1,039,000
Antigua, etc	172,093	3,421,000
Guiana	84,900	4,297,000
Mauritius	68,600	2,113,000
Cape of Good Hope	38,400	1,247,000
Total	780,993	£20,000,000

Such has been the story of freedom on other continents under the Union Jack. Let us see how its story compares with that of other flags upon the continents of America.

The stories of the flag of Mexico and of the republics of South America are so changing and unsettled that they may not be counted in the consideration, and the flag of Spain in Cuba has not yet become an exponent of freedom. The sole competitor for the title of "the flag of the free" is the Stars and Stripes of the United States of North America.

The colonies in North America were, at the

---

* Extract from Dictionary of Statistics, p. 541, "Abolition of Slavery":

time of Lord Mansfield's decision, in 1772, colonies of the British crown, and moved, no doubt, by emulation with their brothers in Great Britain, and desiring to follow their example, the representatives of those colonies met at Philadelphia, on 27th September, 1774, and in "Continental Congress declared against the slave-trade, and forbade further importation into British America." They were then loyal supporters of the Union Jack, and, following its ideals, made a step in the right direction.

It was, no doubt, in imitation of this spirit of British freedom that their Declaration of Independence (4th July, 1776), stated, "We hold these truths to be self-evident, that all men are created equal; that they are endowed by their Creator with certain unalienable rights; that among these are life, liberty and the pursuit of happiness."

Yet, at the very time when they claimed that all men were born equal, well nigh a million blacks were held by them in bondage,* and this sounding "declaration of liberty" did not bring freedom to a single slave.

---

* In 1780, there were 1,191,000 slaves in the United States, and, as late as 1860, more than 4,000,000.

Indeed, when eleven years afterwards, in 1787, the representatives of the thirteen States met* in federal convention, and adopted the Constitution of the United States, the existence of slavery under their flag was recognized and its continuance guaranteed.

They were evidently conscious of the fact that the statements of their " Declaration " were not in harmony with their actions, and therefore the provisions in their " Constitution " concerning slavery were stated in a veiled and subtle way, the words "slave" and "slavery" being carefully excluded. In this way the clauses of the American constitution were intentionally framed to be capable of a different interpretation from that which their wording would apparently convey.†

In the article‡ which regulated the apportionment of representation between the several States, a basis of enumeration is arranged.

" Representatives shall be apportioned among the several States which may be in-

---

* 25th May, 1787, at Philadelphia.

† A peculiarity which has reappeared in many subsequent treaties of the United States.

‡ Article I., Section 3, Constitution of United States, 1787.

cluded within this Union according to their respective numbers, which shall be determined by adding to the whole number of free persons, including those bound to service for a term of years, and excluding Indians not taxed, three-fifths of all other persons."

By the words "all other persons" were meant the slaves, who, although they were not given votes, were counted in determining the number of representatives to be elected by the State in which they were held.

The leaven of English freedom had continued to work among some of the States after their separation from the Crown, and emancipation had been begun in Vermont in 1777, in Pennsylvania in 1780, and was impending in some of the others, but had by no means been accepted in all.*

As slavery was legal in some of the States and illegal in others, it also became necessary, in order to gain the acceptance of the union by these latter States, that a clause guaranteeing the rendition of fugitive slaves should be embodied in the constitution. It was therefore enacted:

---

* Emancipation was effected in New Jersey, 1804; New York, 1827.

"No person held to service or labour in one State under the laws thereof, escaping to another, shall, in consequence of any law or regulation therein, be disharged from such service or labour, but shall be delivered up on claim of the party to whom such service may be due."*

It is stated on the authority of Madison, † "the father of the constitution," that the word used in each case in the original draft was "servitude," but it was changed to the word "service."

The expulsion of the words, although it might appear better to the eye, did not alter the fact that the whole of the United States, which then framed their union, although they did not all practise slavery, yet every one of them then consented to its perpetuation, and thus it existed legally under the Stars and Stripes from 1787 until 1865, when happily it was terminated.‡

Such is the story of the slave's "freedom" under the flag of the United States.

---

* Article IV., section 2, Constitution of United States, 1787.

† James Madison, subsequently twice President of the United States, 1809 and 1813.

‡ Constitutional amendment abolishing slavery, 31st January, 1865.

What has been the story of his freedom under the Union Jack in Canada?

We have seen that slavery, excepting on the soil of Great Britain, was not abolished in all other parts of the British Empire until 1833, and not in the United States until 1865. In 1792 self-government had been granted to Canada, and, under the two-crossed Jack, at the first meetings which were held by the parliament in Upper Canada, slavery was abolished on 9th July, 1793.* This was before the creation, in 1801, of our present Jack.

In Canada alone, of all the outer American lands over which the flag has been displayed, beginning from the very day on which it first was raised, this three-crossed Jack has always proclaimed freedom to the slave.

Canada in such way has added honour to this flag, and made it more particularly her own; for on the continent of America, whether he came from the British West Indies, from the southern continent, from Cuba or the United States, in all of which he was still

---

* There are some isolated instances of slaves who continued in the possession of their previous owners, but after this date any slave brought to the country, and every child born, was free.

the chattel of his owner, so soon as the slave reached the soil of Canada, and came under the colours of "our" Union Jack, that moment he was free.

The deep significance which this early law of Canada had given to the flag has often been attested by coloured men before their fellow-citizens and the world, and particularly by Frederick Douglas, the great coloured orator of the United States. While dilating upon the great advantage which had come to his own people since freedom had at last been granted to them in the United States, he would contrast their condition in the neighbouring Canadian land, where the black child sat in the public schools by the side of his little white brother, or travelled with him in the same carriage on the trains, and where the law was administered with impartiality for both white and black alike.*

---

* Speaking in the Exposition Hall, at the Columbian Exhibition, Chicago, on 25th August, 1893, Douglas said of his people: "To-day we number 8,000,000 (coloured) people in the United States. To-day a desperate effort is being made to blacken the character of the negro and to brand him as a moral monster. In fourteen States of this Union wild mobs have taken the place of the law. They hang, shoot and burn men of my race without law and without right."

In telling words he would revert to the time when "there was but one flag in America under which the fugitive slave could be secure. When the slave had escaped from the control of his owner and was making his way through the intervening States to the free land of the north, whether he gained the summit of the highest mountains, or hid in the recesses of the deepest valleys, the fugitive could find no safe resting place. If he mingled in the teeming throngs of their busiest cities, he feared detection; if he sought solitude on their widest prairies, beneath the silent stars, he was in dread of being tracked; not until he had sighted the red-crossed Jack and crossing the northern lakes, had touched the strand of Canada's shores, could the slave fall upon his knees and know that at last he was a free man."

Thus pure, unsullied in its story, the three-crossed Union Jack of Canada is the only flag on the continent of America which has been always a "flag of liberty" to the slave, and the true "flag of freedom" by which all men, as their birth-right, have been created equal and free. What higher honour could Canadians wish for its blood-red folds?

CHAPTER XIX.

THE UNION JACK OF CANADA THE FLAG OF LIBERTY TO THE PEOPLE.

There is yet the other ideal phase in which the Union Jack of Canada reigns supreme, that of "Liberty to the People." The inborn hope which buds and blossoms in the hearts of a growing people as their energies evolve and circumstances advance, finds its fruitage in the possession of mastery over their own homes, and thus a nation's desire for liberty is concentrated in the absorbing dream of self-government.

It was this spirit which spoke in the old English colonies in America, when they averred in their address to King George III., that they are "being degraded from the pre-eminent rank of *English* freemen."* The position

---

* Address to the King.

of the citizen in their old home-land was their highest ideal of the liberties of a people, and the only one, even in those times, with which they considered comparison could worthily be made.

The history of the Union Jack is connected, as we have seen, not solely with national allegiance, but yet more with parliamentary government; and its parts have been combined to evidence union under representative institutions.

The creation of the constitution of England was not confined to a single date, nor was it the product of the men of a single period, its growth has been spread, like that of its flag, over century after century, as each successive phase of the ideal dream has become harmonized with the existing requirements of its subjects. Formed largely upon precedent and usage, this constitution reflects the current views of the people, and, therefore, it has never been restricted to fixed and invariable form of words.

There are milestones such as Magna Charta, the Petition of Right, the Habeas Corpus Act, the Act of Settlement, and other landmarks that mark the way; but as with the Union

Jack, so too with the liberties of the British form of government, the story of the combinations is not the record of a revolution, but the gradual process of an evolution.

When at the end of the last century our neighbours in the United States framed their separate constitution, which, with the exception of the amendment respecting slavery, remains identically the same, they based it on the usages of that day when responsible government was almost unknown. Creating an elective king under the name of a president, they endowed him with distinct and extensive powers, which, as then, he still exercises largely of his own private will, or only in consultation with a cabinet which is nominated by himself, and whose members are not members of the House of Representatives, nor are they elected by the people.

How entirely he acts without the instructions or the initiation of Congress, was only too evidently shown in the recent Venezuela-Guiana incident, when President Cleveland's message was promulgated with all the unbridled vehemence of an autocrat.[*]

The President of the United States having

---

[*] 1896.

been elected for a definite term of years, represents the opinion prevailing at the time of his election, but no matter how much the opinion of the nation may afterwards change, he continues to rule, until his allotted term shall have expired, even though he be in absolute conflict with the expressed will of the people.

It is true there are provisions in the constitution for checking his course, or for his impeachment, but in cases in which this has been attempted to be enforced, the trial has lasted longer than his term. His appointment having been the result of an election, the President represents not the whole people, but only the political party at the time of his election in the majority.

Being then the party representative of a definite political section, his acts are expected by those who have elected him to be used towards continuing their party in power, and thus the person from time to time holding the position of President becomes a distinct vehicle for the exercise of party political warfare.

This written constitution of the United States, admirable though it may have been at the time, and perhaps an improvement upon the then existing state of things, was born over a century ago in the times of autocratic government, and though thus old and out of date, it has remained ever since practically unchanged.

During this same hundred years, as civilization has advanced, education enlightened the masses, and intelligence expanded among the people, there has grown up that marvellous form of government under which we Canadians live—the British constitutional monarchy. In this British Empire the Queen represents the people, not a party, and is the permanent chairman of the nation. Tempered by her continuous counsel the will of parliament is her will. The ministers of the crown, who form the Executive, are elected by the people, and sit in the same House of Commons with the other elected representatives. Debating with them on the issues of the day, they are responsible to their fellow-members for the measures which they introduce, and when they fail to carry these measures and cease to secure the support of the majority of the people's representatives, then the ministry resigns and is succeeded at the call of the sovereign by a cabinet which shall represent that majority, or, should the matter be of sufficient importance, the whole parliament is forthwith dissolved by the sovereign as the neutral and unbiased centre of impartial power, and the question at issue is quickly submitted for decision by the ballots of the electors. Thus the acts of the premier or chief minister who is head of the executive and of his cabinet, and also of the party of which he is leader, are at once subject to the opinion of the people, without waiting for the completion of their term.*

The Governor-General of Canada does not, as so many of the people of the United States imagine, govern the country, acting with absolute power under the direction of the government of Great Britain, for in every way, except for purposes of Imperial advice and the declaration of war, Canada is practically an independent Dominion. By virtue of his office he represents the person of the Sovereign of the Empire in the local government in this portion of the British realm, and is the con-

---

* The life of a parliament in Canada is limited to five years, and, unless it has been dissolved in the interval, must return for re-election at the end of that term.

necting link between the Mother-parliament in Great Britain and the parliament in the Dominion. As in the Parent-kingdom the sovereign is secured in impartiality by the grace of birth, so in the Daughter-realm the Governor-General is dissociated from all local entanglements by virtue of being appointed from without by the central source of honour and power. His distinctive flag (40) is the "Union Jack," having on its centre the arms of Canada surrounded by a wreath of maple leaves, the emblem of Canada, the whole being surmounted by the Royal crown.

40. FLAG OF THE GOVERNOR-GENERAL OF CANADA.

The flag of the governor or administrator in all other British colonies and dependencies is the Union Jack, having upon it the arms or badge of the colony, surrounded by a green garland of laurel leaves on a white shield. In 1870, as a special honour, the Imperial sanction was given to Canada of placing a garland of maple leaves, instead of laurel, upon the flag of its Governor-General. The Lieutenant-Governors of the provinces of Canada being appointed by the government of the Dominion, their flags bear the arms of their several provinces surrounded by a similar garland of maple leaves but without the crown (41).

41. FLAG OF THE LIEUTENANT-GOVERNOR OF QUEBEC.

In this Governor-General's flag, with its Royal crown, its maple leaf and Canadian coat-of-arms backed up by the Union Jack, is symbolized the existence of British constitutional government in Canada. In this the Queen is the whole Canadian people, and the Premier and his Cabinet are the representatives of the political party for the time being in power. The Cabinet is responsible to parliament for the policy which they introduce, and for which they, as well as all the other members of the parliament, are immediately answerable to the electors who are the original source of their power.

This modern flexible system of constitutional government in Canada, so closely in touch with the people, in contrast with the age-stiffened system in the United States, was neatly brought out by Lord Dufferin during his term as Governor-General of Canada, in a speech he delivered at Toronto, in 1874, after his visit to Chicago.

"More than once," said he, "I was addressed with the playful suggestion that Canada should unite her fortunes with those of the great Republic." (Laughter). "To these invitations I invariably replied by acquainting them that in Canada we were essentially a democratic people (great laughter), that nothing would content us unless the popular will could exercise an immediate and complete control over the executive of the country (renewed laughter), that the ministers who conducted the government were but a committee of parliament, which was in itself an emanation from the constituencies (loud applause), and that no Canadian would be able to breathe freely if he thought the persons administering the affairs of the country were removed beyond the supervision and contact of our legislative assemblies " (cheers).

It is, then, easily seen why Canadians love their Union Jack. It is the signal of parliamentary government by British constitutional principles. It represents progress and modern ideas. The rule of the people, for the people, by the people, through their Queen; and, therefore, it is the evidence of their affectionate and loyal allegiance to that monarchy under whose benign sway Canada, above all other countries on this continent of America, is the land of the free.

CHAPTER XX.

THE UNION FLAG OF THE BRITISH EMPIRE.

The story of the Union Jack as we have thus followed it has told how its allegiance travelled beyond the little islands which it first had claimed as its territory and naturalized its affections upon the soil of this great north land of America.

And not over Canada alone, but also to every colonist in the outer continents, in Australasia and the islands of the sea, and to all the Potentates of mighty India, it bears the same glad story of brotherhood and United Realm.

The Union Jack flying by itself has its special significance. Upon the bowsprit of a ship it is local, at the mast head it is the evidence of the rank of the admiral who bears it, liament, which was in itself an emanation from the constituencies (loud applause), and that no Canadian would be able to breathe freely if he thought the persons administering the affairs of the country were removed beyond the supervision and contact of our legislative assemblies" (cheers).

It is, then, easily seen why Canadians love their Union Jack. It is the signal of parliamentary government by British constitutional principles. It represents progress and modern ideas. The rule of the people, for the people, by the people, through their Queen; and, therefore, it is the evidence of their affectionate and loyal allegiance to that monarchy under whose benign sway Canada, above all other countries on this continent of America, is the land of the free.

CHAPTER XX.

THE UNION FLAG OF THE BRITISH EMPIRE.

The story of the Union Jack as we have thus followed it has told how its allegiance travelled beyond the little islands which it first had claimed as its territory and naturalized its affections upon the soil of this great north land of America.

And not over Canada alone, but also to every colonist in the outer continents, in Australasia and the islands of the sea, and to all the Potentates of mighty India, it bears the same glad story of brotherhood and United Realm.

The Union Jack flying by itself has its special significance. Upon the bowsprit of a ship it is local, at the mast head it is the evidence of the rank of the admiral who bears it, or on shore of the officer who displays it, but combined in the upper corner of a larger ensign it is the flag of the nation, and thus environed becomes the Union Flag.

It is a misnomer to call a flag of this combined shape a Union "Jack," this being the proper name solely for the smaller flag comprising only the three Island crosses, but place this smaller flag of the three Kingdoms in the upper corner of a larger flag and it becomes the sign of identity of allegiance, the emblem of united power and the evidence of the union of British patriotism with the story that may be told by the colourings and forms of the rest of the flag.

The portion of the flag next the staff is termed the *hoist*, and the outer part or length, the *fly*. Another method of description is arrived at by dividing the flag into four quarters or "cantons," two *next the staff* and two *in the fly*.

The Union Jack is used in the upper or "dexter" canton, next the staff, on several distinctive flags.

The White Ensign (Pl. I., fig. 2). A white flag bearing the large red cross of St. George and having the Union Jack in the dexter canton

The Blue Ensign (Pl. I., fig. 3). A blue flag having the Union Jack in the dexter canton.

The Red Ensign (Pl. I., fig. 1). A red flag having the Union Jack in the dexter canton.

The first was won and is worn only by the warships of the British navy, the second is worn only on ships of the navies of British colonies and of the Royal naval reserve,* and the third was won and is worn by all British merchantmen and also on the ships of the Royal navy.

It will be remembered that the red ensign, first with its St. George's cross under Charles II., and afterwards with its two-crossed Union Jack under Queen Anne, had become the national ensign of all British ships at sea, and not being restricted to any particular services, as are the white and blue ensigns, it has extended in its usage and now, with its three-crossed union, become the ensign of the British people on shore as well as afloat.

---

* See Appendix B.

"Where is the Briton's land?
Where'er the blood-red Ensign flies,
There is the Briton's land."

Whether it be in the "right little, tight little islands," of the old land, or in the greater area of the colonies which stud the globe, the presence of this Union Flag proclaims the sovereignty of the united nations.

Thus the three crosses in the Union Jack have ceased to have solely their local meanings, for their story has become merged in the larger significance which their presence now imparts to the universal Imperial flag as being the sign of this greater British union.

This further evolution in the story of the flag has come step by step.

In the century of the expansion of Raleigh's "trade command," the governors of the English colonies, principally of those in America, began giving to their local shipping commissions to engage in the various and free-licensed methods by which that trade was being obtained. Some inconvenience seems to have resulted from this practice.

Under William III. the matter was taken up and an Order in Council passed at Whitehall approving of a suggestion then made by the Lords' Commissioners of the Admiralty.

"Their Excellencies, the Lords' Justices, have been pleased to refer unto us a Report of the Lords' Commissioners of Trade representing the inconveniencies that do attend Merchant ships bearing the King's colours in and among the Plantations abroad under colour of the Commissions given them by his Majesty's Govenors of the said Plantations, do most humbly report to their Excellencies that we do agree with the said Lords' Commissioners for Trade, that all ships to whom the aforesaid Governors shall by the authority lodged in them grant commissions, ought to wear colours that may distinguish them from private ships as is done by those employed by the Officers of the Navy, Ordnance, Victualling and others, and therefore do humbly propose, that all the said Governors may be directed to oblige the Commanders of such Merchant Ships to which they grant commissions to wear no other Jack than that hereafter mentioned, namely, that worn by His Majesty's Ships, with the distinction of a white Escutcheon in the middle thereof, and that the said mark of Distinction may extend itself to one half of the depth of the Jack and one third part of the Fly thereof, according to the sample herewith annexed.*

The white escutcheon of the home departmental flags thus extended itself to the English Jacks used in the colonies.

42. AUSTRALIAN EMBLEMS.

The governors or high commissioners, or administrators of British colonies and dependencies, were afterwards authorized to place upon this white escutcheon on the Union Jack the arms or badge of the colony in which they served. In this way it has come that the arms of *Canada*, the Southern Cross constellation of *Queensland*, the red cross and British lion of *Victoria*, the black swan of *Western Australia* (42), and the other special distinctive emblems in each of the

---

* Order-in-Council, Whitehall, July 31st, 1701.

British colonies are now displayed upon the flags of the governor's in each.

In 1865, when colonial navies were first established, the vessels of war maintained by the local governments were authorized to use the blue ensign, with the seal or badge of the colony in the centre of the fly,* and thus the escutcheon was given another position, and the local stories of the Australian colonies, which established these fleets, became embodied in the British blue ensign.† A similar privilege, although they are not commissioned as vessels of war, was afterwards extended to the fishery protection cruisers of Canada, so that on these and all other vessels which are owned by the Dominion Government, the blue ensign is carried with the arms of Canada in the centre of the fly (Pl. IX., fig. 2).

By these successive steps the Imperial idea became attached to one of the ensigns of the British navy.

From the plain white escutcheon in the centre of the Union Jack, 1701, to the special emblem in the fly of the blue ensign, 1865,

---

* "Colonial Defences Act," 23 Victoria, Cap. 14.
† Warrant of the Lords' Commissioners of the Admiralty.

was a long way, but yet other steps were to be taken.

The vessels owned by the governments of the colonies had thus been given their special British flags, but provision had not been made for those owned by private citizens. The plain red ensign is worn without distinction by all British subjec's on all lands and seas. As the colonists developed in native energy so their merchant shipping increased, and in recognition of this all colonial owned merchant vessels were accorded in 1889* the right of wearing, *together* with the red ensign, an *additional* flag on which might be shown the distinguishing badge of their colony. In order to prevent the possibility of mistakes in identification it was further directed that any flags of this character were to be made in such a way as not to resemble any of the existing flags of the Royal navy.

In some of the colonies in Australasia local flags of excellent design have been devised, but these "additional" and "separate" flags are not all that can be desired, for while the local flag might give expression to the local patriotism represented, there

---

* Merchant Shipping (Colours) Act, 1889.

comes with it also an idea of separation, and it does not succeed in expressing the dominant and prevailing sentiment of allegiance to

One Queen, One Empire, One Flag!

It has fallen to the lot of the statesmen of Canada, who do not seem to be behindhand in developing new and Imperial ideas, to suggest another step in the history of the ensign.

The merchant shipping of Canada stands fifth in rank in merchant shipping among the nations of the world.

The government ships were authorized to use the blue ensign with the arms of Canada as their distinguishing flag, but the merchant marine used the same plain red ensign as worn by the merchant marine of Great Britain, and as no special colonial flag had been adopted for Canada, her merchant ships could not be recognized amidst those of the Mother country.

In 1892, to meet this requirement, the Lords' Commissioners of the Admiralty, on the suggestion of the Canadian Department of Marine, issued a warrant permitting the

---

*The order is British (Home Kingdom), United States, German, French, Canadian.

badge of the arms of Canada to be inserted in the fly of the red ensign as well as in the blue, and this new combined red ensign was empowered to be used by all citizens of Canada.*

Thus was formed the union flag of Canada.

The Ensign of Canada (Pl. ix., fig. 1) is the British red ensign, having the Union Jack in the dexter canton and the arms of Canada in the fly.

Like the expansion of the British constitution to patriot governments beyond the seas so has come the extension step by step of the old union flag to the newly-created colonies. As the spirit of that constitution has been adapted to the local circumstances in each so the red ensign, which is the embodiment of the power and glory of the British nation, has been emblazoned with the local fervour of each young and growing people, who fervently loving their own new land stand unconquerably in union with the Motherland and rejoice at seeing their own emblem set upon the Mother flag.

Such a flag, such a real flag, tells its grand story in a way that a national flag ought to

---

*Admiralty Warrant, Feb. 2nd, 1892.

do, for the red ensign of the Homeland with the signal of the colony added to its folds in each far-off land signals to the beholder that it is the *Union Flag of the British Empire.*

When the Canadian sees the Union Crosses displayed in the top corner on his Canadian ensign it speaks to him not only as his own native flag but yet more as his sign of brotherhood in an Empire wider than his own home, broader than the continent on which he lives, for it is the visible evidence of his citizenship in the Empire of Great and Greater Britain.

The fervid eloquence of Daniel Webster in 1834 described that Empire as "a power dotted over the surface of the whole Globe with her possessions and military posts; whose morning drum beat following the sun and keeping company with the hours, circles the earth with one continuous and unbroken strain of the martial airs of England."*

If this heart-rousing testimony of the majesty of the Empire, of which we Canadians form a part, had been given by one of ourselves, it might have been tinged with the suspicion of self-glorious boasting, but springing from the lips of so distinguished a citizen

---

* Speech May 7th, 1834.

of the United States, its fervid utterance is the candid acknowledgment of a nation greater than his own, whose grandeur compelled his admiration.

If over half a century ago this admission was true, how much more so is it at the present day.

Those " possessions " which fired the statesman's imagination have marvellously increased, that "power" has expanded beyond his utmost dreams. Since that time no nation, not even his own, has progressed like ours has. Canada then lost to him in the solitude of far-off forests or of pathless plain, has arisen like a young lion and gripped the American continent from sea to sea, carrying the Union Jack in continuous line of government from shore to shore. Australia has risen beneath the Southern Star; India in itself became an Empire, and Africa, youngest born of all the lion's brood, is welding fast another continent beneath the Imperial sway.

These are the nations of the Union Jack; the galaxy of parliaments of free men which has arisen round the Central Isles and the throne of Her who, with her statesmen, "knew the seasons when to take occasion by the hand and make the bounds of freedom wider yet."

In this Nation of nations, Canadians join hands with their brothers around the world, and raise aloft the Union Jack in the Imperial flag as the glad ensign of their united allegiance, a union for which Canadians, as much as any, have proved their faith and ever stand in foremost rank ready and willing to defend.

There is something marvellous in the world-wide influence of this three-crossed flag of the parent nation, whose sons have followed its ideals through all the centuries. Sometimes they have made mistakes, but undaunted, masterful and confident, have profited by the hard won experience, and progressing with the march of time find at the close of this nineteenth century that they "have builded better than they knew."

Thus when in the opening month of 1896 Britain stood alone, as said a Canadian statesman,* in *"splendid isolation,"* there was heard coming not only from Canada, but from every

---

* Hon. W. E. Foster, Minister of Finance of Canada, speech in the House of Commons, Ottawa.

Daughter nation around the seas, the same brave refrain which had been sung by a Canadian poet in the stirring Mason and Slidell times of 1861.

> "When recent danger threatened near,
> We nerved our hearts to play our part,
> Not making boast, nor feeling fear;
> But as the news of insult spread,
> Were none to dally or to lag;
> For all the grand old island spirit
> Which Britain's chivalrous sons inherit
> Was roused, and as one heart, one hand,
> We rallied round our flag."

Such, then, is the story, such is the meaning of our Union Jack: the emblem of combined constitutional government, the proclaimer of British liberty, the Union sign of British rule.

Mindful of its story, happy in their lot, facing the world, its sons encircle the earth with their glad anthem

God save Victoria, Queen and Empress.

THE END.

APPENDIX A.

A PLEA FOR THE MAPLE LEAF.

The multi-coloured quarterings of the Dominion arms, as shown on the shield upon the Canadian ensign, have not been found entirely efficient, for they fail in being easily recognizable.

Flags are signals to be used for conveying information to persons at a distance; their details should, therefore, be simple in form and be displayed in simple colours.

The cross on the Swiss flag and the shield on the Italian flag, though small, are easily recognized ; but the coat-of-arms on the Canadian flag is, even when near, an indistinguishable medley.

Several suggestions for improvement have been made, but we would join with many others in a plea for the maple leaf.

The maple tree is found in luxuriance in every province of the Dominion. Varieties of it grow, it is true, in other parts of America; but the tree is in its greatest glory in the northern zones, where throughout Canada, extended along her line of similar latitude, it attains to its most robust and greatest development. It flourishes in Newfoundland, in the Maritime Provinces and in Quebec. It is the finest forest tree in Ontario. A wreath of Manitoba maple leaves was placed upon the statue of Sir John Macdonald as the votive offering of the North-West, and anyone who has seen the giant maple leaves of British Columbia will say the maple leaf is the natural emblem of Canada.

As well as being the natural emblem, it is also the typical emblem. It was held in high esteem by the early settlers of Quebec, and was adopted, in 1836, as the French-Canadian emblem for the festival of St. Jean Baptste. It was placed on the coinage of New Brunswick early in the century, and a whole maple tree was shown on the coinage of Prince Edward Island before the time of Confederation. At the creation of the union in Confederation it was placed in the arms of Quebec and of Ontario, and was heraldically recognized as the emblem of Canada.

Maple leaves form the wreaths on the flag of the Governor-General of the Dominion and on the flags of the Lieutenant-Governors of all the provinces. It was the emblem placed by His Royal Highness the Prince of Wales on the colours of the "Royal Canadians," the 100th Regiment, raised in Canada in 1865, and is still worn as the regimental badge of their successors, the Royal Leinster Regiment. It is on the North-West medals of 1885, and on the uniform and accoutrements of the Canadian Infantry and of the North-West Mounted Police.

It has revelled in poetry and prose; it is the theme of the songs of our children; and the stirring strains of "The Maple Leaf" form an accompaniment to our British national anthem.

It has been worn on the breasts of all the representative champions of Canada—at the oar, on the yachts, on the athletic fields, in military contests and at the rifle ranges—as the emblem of their country.

Everywhere throughout the world the maple leaf has won recognition as the emblem of Canadians, and may well be displayed upon their flag.

As to the colour. Green is the emblem of youth and vigour, and if, instead of the Dominion arms, the green maple leaf were placed on the shield of the Canadian ensign, the flag would be fairer to see and more easily distinguished. Or if the colour used were scarlet, the colour of courage, then both the natural and emblematic attributes of the leaf would still be represented.

This introduction of the maple leaf has often been suggested, but if in this year of the Diamond Jubilee of our gracious Queen a white diamond of one-third the size of the "Union" was substituted for the shield, then indeed we should have a flag (Pl. IX., No. 3) which would signalize an historic epoch, and be one which could be known at a glance among all others.

The green maple leaf on the white diamond in the

fly of the red ensign would tell as bravely and more clearly the story of the "coat of-arms" on the shield, but it would also be a national tribute to that Queen, under whose commanding influence the colonies have arisen around the Empire, and be a record of that Diamond Jubilee of Victoria which has been the revelation of their union and the united testimony of their affectionate allegiance.

APPENDIX B.

CANADIAN WAR MEDALS.

The War Medal (38) was granted in 1848, to be worn by the men of the British forces who had served in the fleets and armies during the wars from 1793 to 1814. Among these the Canadian militia were included.

Clasps were granted to those men who had been present at the actions of St. Sebastian, Vittoria, Salamanca, Talavera and Vimiera in the Peninsular campaign; and in the Canadian campaign, for the actions at Fort Detroit, 16th August, 1812; Chateauguay, 26th October, 1813, and Chrystler's Farm, 11th November, 1813.

The medal from which the drawing is made is engraved, A. Wilcox, Canadian militia, and bears the clasp, Fort Detroit.

The North-West Canada medal (39), was granted in 1886 to all who had served in the Canadian North-West in 1885. The clasp "Saskatchewan" was granted to all who were present at the actions of Fish Creek, 24th April; Batoche, 12th May, and Frenchman's Butte, 27th May, 1885.

The forces serving in the expedition of 1885 were drawn entirely from the Canadian militia and North-West mounted police, with the addition of the officers of the Imperial forces who were associated in command.

APPENDIX C.

A SAMPLE CANADIAN RECORD.

The service record of the Nelles family of Hamilton gives some idea of the calls to military service in Canada:

Great grandfather, on British side, in 1776.
Grandfather, in War of 1812.
Father, in Rebellion of 1837.
Son, Fenian Invasion, 1866.
Nephew, North-West, 1885.

www.ingramcontent.com/pod-product-compliance
Lightning Source LLC
Chambersburg PA
CBHW020759230426
43666CB00007B/759